T0325075

SURVEY

OF

ADVANCED

MICROPROCESSORS

SURVEY OF ADVANCED MICROPROCESSORS

Andrew M. Veronis, Ph. D.
Professor
Department of Computer Science
University of Maryland, Eastern Shore
and
Whiting School of Engineering
The Johns Hopkins University

VNR **SPRINGER SCIENCE+BUSINESS MEDIA, LLC**

Library of Congress Catalog Card Number 90-21750
ISBN 978-0-442-00120-9

Library of Congress Cataloging-in-Publication Data

Veronis, Andrew.
    Survey of advanced microprocessors / Andrew Veronis.
        p.   cm.
    Includes index.
    ISBN 978-0-442-00120-9   ISBN 978-1-4615-3930-8 (eBook)
    DOI 10.1007/978-1-4615-3930-8
    1. Microprocessors.   2. Computer architecture   I. Title.
    QA76.5.V48   1991
    004.2'2--dc20   90-21750
                                                                      CIP

This book is dedicated to my wife Elizabeth.

Preface

Microprocessors have come a long way since their conception. They have become formidable processing tools, and we encounter them in almost every part of our daily activities, from the kitchen with its microwave oven to the cockpit of a sophisticated aircraft.

The purposes of this book are to "walk through" the current microprocessor technology and briefly to describe some of the most advanced microprocessors available. The book is a survey of advanced microprocessors, aimed particularly at the engineering manager rather than the design engineer.

Chapter One outlines the history of microprocessors and describes some terminology used in computer architecture.

Chapter Two discusses advanced computer concepts, such as data and data types, addressing modes, pipelining, and cache memory.

Chapter Three describes new computer architectures, such as reduced-instruction-set computers (RISCs) and very-long-instruction-word computers. RISC architecture has become very popular among designers.

Chapter Four discusses an architecture, data-flow, which is a departure from the conventional von Neumann architecture. NEC has applied the dataflow architecture on the design of a very sophisticated image processing chip, the NEC PD7281.

Chapters Five and Six are case studies, describing the Am29000 and the Transputer, respectively.

Chapter Seven describes microprocessors specifically designed for digital signal processing.

Chapter Eight discusses micromultiprocessing and describes the various topologies currently used.

Contents

SURVEY

OF

ADVANCED

MICROPROCESSORS

Chapter 1
Introduction

THE HISTORY OF MICROPROCESSORS

The transistor and the integrated circuit are among the fundamental discoveries in electronics. To date, however, the most significant invention may be the microprocessor.

"Announcing a New Era in Integrated Electronics," Intel advertised its first microprocessor in November 1971. The prophesy already has been fulfilled with delivery of the 8008 in 1972, the 8080 in 1974, the 8085 in 1976, the 8086 in 1978, the 80286 in 1983–84, the 80386 in 1986, and, more recently, the i860 and i960. When this book is published, Intel will have introduced the 80486.

During this interval, throughput has improved 100-fold, the price of a microprocessor has declined from $500 to $5, and the availability of microprocessors has revolutionized design concepts in countless applications. Microcomputers have entered our homes, offices, and automobiles. A four-transputer board (described later), plugged into a personal computer, will yield the same performance as a much larger VAX 8600.

In the late 1960s, it became clear that the practical use of large-scale integrated circuits depended on defining chips to have:

- a high gate-to-pin ratio;

- a regular cell structure; and

- a large standard-part market.

Intel Corporation was formed, in 1968, to exploit the semiconductor memory market with circuits that fulfilled these criteria. Easy semiconductor read-write memories (RAM), read-only memories

1

(ROM), and shift registers were welcomed wherever small memories were needed, particularly in calculators and CRT terminals.

In 1969, Intel engineers began to study ways by which to integrate and partition the control functions of these systems into LSI chips.At the same time, other companies (notably Texas Instruments) explored ways to reduce the time needed to develop custom integrated circuits.

An alternative approach envisioned a customer's application as a computer system that required a control program, i/o monitoring, and arithmetic routines, rather than as a collection of special-purpose logic chips. Intel drew on its strength in memory to partition systems into RAM, ROM, and single controller chips — i.e., CPU.

Intel embarked on the design of two customer-sponsored microprocessors — the 4004 for a calculator and the 8008 for a CRT terminal. The 4004 replaced six chips usable by only one customer. Since the first microcomputer applications were known and easy to understand, instruction sets and architectures were defined in a matter of weeks. As programmable computers, their uses could be extended indefinitely.

The 4004 and the 8008 are both complete CPU on a chip and have similar characteristics, but, because the 4004 was designed for serial BCD arithmetic and the 8008 for 8-bit character handling, their instruction sets are different.

Computer Terminal Corporation (subsequently known as Datapoint) contracted for Intel to make a pushdown stack chip for a processor to be used in a CRT terminal. Datapoint intended to build a bit-serial processor in TTL logic, using shift register memory. Intel counterproposed that the entire processor could be implemented on one chip. This processor was to become the 8008 and, along with the 4004, was to be fabricated using PMOS, the then current memory-fabrication technology. Due to the long lead time that Intel required, Datapoint marketed its serial processor, and, thus, compatibility constraints were imposed on the 8008.

Datapoint specified most of the instruction set and register organization. Intel modified the instruction set so that the processor would fit on one chip and added instructions to make the device more "general purpose," for, although Intel was developing the 8008 for a specific customer, the company wanted the option of selling the chip to others. Since, in those days, Intel was using only 16- and 18-pin packages, the company chose to use 18 pins for the 8008, rather than design a new package for a supposedly low-volume chip.

The 8008 architecture is quite simple compared with those of today's microprocessors. The data-handling facilities provide for byte data only. The memory space is limited to 16 kilobytes, and the stack (small memory area for the temporary storage of data) is on the chip and holds only eight data items. The instruction set is small but symmetrical, with only a few operand addressing modes available. An interrupt mechanism is provided, but there is no way to disable interrupts.

The chip supports eight 8-bit input ports and 24 8-bit output ports. The instruction set can address each port directly. The chip's designers had felt that output ports were more important than input ports, which always could be multiplexed by external hardware under control of additional output ports.

One of the interesting things about the advent of the microprocessor era is that, for the first time, users were given access to the memory bus and could define their own memory structure. No longer were users confined to what vendors offered, as users had been with minicomputers. A user had, for example, the option of putting i/o ports inside a memory address (memory-mapped i/o) inste d of a separate i/o space (direct i/o).

The 8008 contains two register files and four 1-bit flap₃ (carry, parity, sign, and zero). The register files are the scratchpad and address stack.

The scratchpad contains an 8-bit accumulator (A) and six additional 8-bit registers (B, C, D, E, H, and L). All of the arithmetic operations use the accumulator as one of the operands and the memory for the result, as is typical in 8-bit microprocessors. All seven registers can be used interchangeably for on-chip temporary storage.

The instruction set of the 8008 consists of scratchpad-register instructions, accumulator-specific instructions, transfer-of-control instructions, i/o instructions, and processor-control instructions.

By 1973, memory-fabrication technology had advanced from PMOS to NMOS. As an engineering exercise, Intel used the 8008 layout masks with the NMOS process, to obtain increased operating speeds and, after a short study, determined that a new layout was required. The company decided to enhance the processor at the same time and to utilize a new 40-pin package, made practicable for high-volume calculator chips. The result was the 8080 processor.

The 8080 was the first processor specifically designed for the microprocessor market. The chip was constrained to include all of the 8008 instructions, although not necessarily with the same op-codes. Thus, a user's software was portable, but the ROM chips that contained the firmware required replacement. The main objectives in the design of the 8080 were a 10-to-1 improvement in throughput, elimination of many of the then-apparent shortcomings of the 8008, and provision of processing capabilities not found in the 8008. These capabilities included the handling of 16-bit data types (mainly for address calculations) and BCD arithmetic, enhancement of addressing modes, and improvement of interrupt processing.

The lower price of memory chips had made larger memory capacity more practicable. Thus, another goal was the addressing of more than 16K bytes. Symmetry, however, was not a goal, as the benefits of symmetrical extension could not justify the resultant increase in chip size and opcode space.

The 8080 contains a file of seven 8-bit, general-purpose registers, a 16-bit program counter, a 16-bit stack pointer, and five 1-bit flags.

The registers in the 8080 are the same seven 8-bit registers in the 8008 scratchpad. To handle 16-bit data, however, certain 8080 instructions operate on register pairs BC, DE, and HL.

The seven registers can be used interchangeably for on-chip temporary storage. The three register pairs can be used for address manipulations, but their roles are not interchangeable; an 8080 instruction allows operations on DE but not BC. There are address modes that access memory indirectly through BC and DE but not through HL.

The A register serves as the accumulator. The HL pair is used as a memory pointer.

The 8080 has a total memory-access capacity of 64K. The stack is contained in memory, rather than on the chip, to remove the restriction of only seven levels of nested subroutines. The entries on the stack are 16 bits wide. The 16-bit stack pointer is used to locate the stack in memory. The execution of a "call" instruction causes the contents of the program counter to be "pushed" onto the stack, and the "return" instruction causes the last stack entry to be "popped" into the program counter. The stack pointer contains addresses that lead toward the lower end of memory (hence the term *pushdown stack*). This action simplifies both indexing into the stack from the user's program (positive indexing) and displaying the contents of the stack from a front panel.

A programmer can access the stack pointer in the 8080 directly, unlike the 8008. Furthermore, the stack itself is directly accessible, and instructions enable a programmer to push and pop 16-bit items onto the stack.

A couple of flags were added to the 8080 processor status code — i.e., the auxiliary carry flag, useful in BCD arithmetic, and the overflow flag.

Expanded input-output instructions allow the contents of any of the 256 8-bit ports to be transferred either to or from the accumulator. Nonetheless, the bottlenecking weakness inherent in uniprocessors, particularly ones that use registers dedicated to specific tasks, is here. Although the 8080 is better than its predecessor the 8008, it still uses the A register for both i/o and arithmetic operations and, thus, precludes concurrency of these operations.

By 1976, technological advances allowed Intel to consider enhancement of the 8080. Among the several weaknesses in the 8080 are the use of a triple power supply and the need for both an oscillator chip and a system controller chip. The company set out to produce a processor that would operate with a single power supply and would require fewer, if any, support chips. The resultant processor was called the 8085 and was constrained to be machine-code compatible with the 8080. Thus, extensions to the instruction set could use only 12 unused opcodes of the 8080.

Closer examination of the so-called enhanced 8085 reveals that its internal organization does not differ substantially from that of the 8080. The chips have the same register sets and the same flags. A couple of new instructions (Set Interrupt Mask and Reset Interrupt Mask) had been added. The only significant enhancements are the use of an on-chip oscillator and the use of a single power supply. Several new instructions that had been included never were announced because of their ramifications on the 8085 support software and because of the compatibility constraints that the instructions would have imposed on the forthcoming 8086.

The 8086, a processor with a 16-bit-wide data structure, was designed to provide an order-of-magnitude increase over both the 8080 and the 8085. The processor was to be compatible with the 8080 at the assembly language level, so that existing 8080 software could be reassembled and correctly executed on the 8086. Therefore, the 8080 register set and instruction set were to appear as logical subsets of the 8086 registers and instructions. By utilizing a general-register structure, Intel could capitalize on its experience with the 8080 to obtain a processor with the highest degree of sophistication. Strict 8080 compatibility, however, was not attempted, especially in areas where compatibility would have compromised the final design.

The organization of the 8086 processor comprises a memory structure, a register structure, an instruction set, and an external interface. The processor can access up to one megabyte of memory and up to 64K input-output ports. By today's microprocessor standards, these capabilities do not seem significant, but they were when the 8086 was introduced in the mid-1970s.

The 8086 uses "segmented" addressing; that is, memory is divided into 64K byte segments, and referencing of a datum inside a segment is accomplished by the addition of an address and the contents of a segment register. The problems arising from segmented addressing are discussed in Chapter 2.

The 8086 contains a total of 13 16-bit registers and 9 1-bit flags. The registers are divided into three files of four registers each. The 13th register, called the *instruction pointer*, is not directly accessible by a programmer; this register is manipulated with control-transfer instructions. One cannot help but notice the compatibility of the 8086 register set with those of the 8080/8085.

The 8086 processor has seen days of glory since IBM decided to use a subset, the 8088, as well as an enhanced version, the 80286, in the IBM line of personal computers. Many IBM-compatible personal computers, called *clones*, followed suit.

Intel microprocessors were chosen for description as a tribute to the first manufacturer of these marvels of technology. Other semiconductor manufacturers, however, did not stand idle. Zilog, a company formed by former Intel engineers, produced the Z80, which outsold every other 8-bit microprocessor on the market. The Z80, an enhanced version of the 8080, is upward-compatible with the latter; that is, it can execute code written for the 8080, but it also has its own additional instructions.

Motorola, another semiconductor pioneer, came out with a full line of 8-bit and 16-bit microprocessors. The Motorola 68000 family of microprocessors offers several advantages over the 8086 processor.

The Motorola 68020 is a true 32-bit microprocessor. This processor has 16 32-bit, general-purpose registers, a 32-bit program counter, a 16-bit status register, a 32-bit vector base register, two 32-bit alternate function code registers, and two 32-bit cache-memory-handling registers. The 68020 can manipulate bit, byte, 16-bit, 32-bit, and 64-bit operands. The direct-addressing capacity of this chip is four gigabytes!

Another line of microprocessors is the bit-slice device. Some of these devices offer definite advantages but have not become as popular as the other microprocessors.

Microprocessors also have given us the tools with which to produce multimicroprocessor systems, such as the Hypercube and the Connection Machine. These types of systems can meet the demand for additional computing power to satisfy new requirements and to support complex applications.

The demand for faster and more sophisticated microprocessors has led to continued enhancement of microprocessor internal organizations.

ADVANCED MICROPROCESSORS

As the number of applications with more elaborate computational demands increases, more processing power is needed. This need can be met, at the processor level, by relying on technological improvements to push the microprocessor beyond its current maximum capabilities or, at the system level, by extending the capabilities of a single microprocessor through concurrent execution.

Bottlenecking, which is inherent in von Neumann-type processors, is minimized through the use of pipelining.

The demand for more enhanced microprocessors and the technological improvements of very-large-scale integration have led to introduction of new microprocessors. A new type of organization, called reduced-instruction-set computer (RISC), was designed and prototyped at the University of California at Berkeley.

The RISC architecture is a radical departure from conventional thinking about microprocessor design. This type of design includes four important constraints. The execution time is one instruction per cycle. Instructions are intended to be as simple and fast as microinstructions on computers like the VAX and, to simplify implementation, also have the same size. To simplify system design, system memory is accessed only with LOAD and STORE instructions. This feature is well matched for a microprocessor optimized for keeping operands in internal registers. Finally, the RISC design epitomizes support of high-level languages.

Several microprocessor manufacturers have adopted the RISC architecture.

Other enhancements are the departure from the control-flow, von Neumann-type architecture and the introduction of the so-called data-flow architecture.

Sophisticated microcontrollers and dedicated digital-signal-processing microprocessors are now available. Texas Instruments markets a microprocessor with LISP on the chip. Intel markets the i860, which, according to the company, "delivers supercomputing performance in a single VLSI component" – a supercomputer on a chip. This processor uses a new architecture called very-long-instruction-word (VLIW), which, some claim, will replace RISC. The i860 is described in a later chapter.

The i960, a microprocessor designed for embedded applications, displays a lot of the features of the ill-fated 432.

INMOS markets the Transputer, a 32-bit microprocessor

designed with parallel processing in mind.

Thus, the simple 4-bit microprocessor of the early 1970s has grown into a respectable computer, competing very successfully and, in several areas, surpassing the performance of some superminis and mainframes. Today's microprocessors are fast, access an abundant amount of memory, and are supported by a vast number of high-level languages. The future of advanced microprocessors appears to be very bright.

Several enhancements of the so-called advanced microprocessors over the early devices can be identified.

First is the addition of more general-purpose, undedicated registers. A large number of registers reduce the number of times that a processor must access external memory. Thus, a requirement for the proper design of the RISC architecture is the availability of a significant number of registers.

Second is the larger size of data and address paths. Advanced microprocessors directly access a far larger memory spectrum than 8-bit counterparts.

Third is the increased speed of execution through the application of such techniques as pipelining and overlapping and microprogrammed control units. Furthermore, the circuitry of the system clock has been enhanced to allow operating speeds of 10–35 MHz.

Fourth is the more enhanced addressing modes.

Fifth is the availability of various memory-management techniques. The capability of supporting cache memory now is available to most advanced microprocessors.

Sixth is the usability of advanced microprocessors in various multiprocessing topologies.

A seventh, and highly debated, enhancement is larger instruction sets, which proponents believe render a microprocessor more powerful. Others are strong proponents of the RISC approach.

TERMINOLOGY

Various terms are used throughout this text to describe the enhancements that have been implemented in microprocessors. Some of these terms have created a certain amount of controversy, while others have created a certain amount of confusion. The interpretations of these terms given in this book are not necessarily unique; these interpretations have been more or less accepted as standard among the industry.

The terms *organization* and *architecture* were used in this chapter indiscriminately. These two terms, however, have created many an argument among the experts. Their description here is desirable.

The term *organization* defines the act of arranging something into a coherent unit, and the term *architecture* defines the art of designing and building a structure. At least, these are two formal definitions provided in a dictionary. In computer engineering and computer science, however, the definitions of these two terms are rather vague, due to lack of standardization.

For some, architecture refers to the interface that a machine language programmer sees; this view includes user-visible registers and data types and their formats and instruction sets. For others, computer architecture is a subset of computer system organization. For yet others, computer organization is a subset of computer architecture.

On the basis of the latter definition, the diagram in Fig. 1–1 can be drawn.

Application architecture is the interface between an application program and a high-level programming language plus operating system. Most application programs are written in standard programming languages, such as C, FORTRAN, or Pascal, and most are designed to execute on standard operating systems, such as UNIX. The language specification and operating-system calls define the application architecture.

Instruction set architecture refers to the interface between an assembly language program and the computer hardware. The architecture is defined by the registers, instruction formats, and addressing modes of a processor.

Internal architecture is defined by the gates, buses, memory, and execution units of a processor. Normally, this architecture is invisible to user-supplied programs, but has a great bearing on performance.

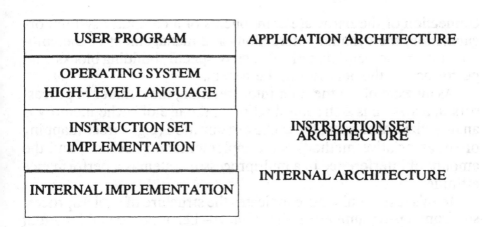

Fig. 1-1. Architecture diagrammed

Flynn [1] classifies computer architectures by the properties of data and instruction streams. The following four categories of computers evolve from this somewhat outdated classification:

DATA STREAM

SINGLE-INSTRUCTION SINGLE-DATA	SINGLE-INSTRUCTION MULTIPLE-DATA	
MULTIPLE-INSTRUCTION SINGLE-DATA	MULTIPLE-INSTRUCTION MULTIPLE-DATA	INSTRUCTION STREAM

Jean-Loup Baer [2] provides another interpretation of the term *architecture*, not relating the term to any programming attributes. Baer regards computer architecture as encompassing structure, organization, implementation, and performance. Structure is the interconnection of the hardware components of a computer system; organization, the dynamic interactions and management of the components; implementation, the design of specific building blocks; and performance, the behavior of the system.

As an example of the Baer interpretation, the number of processors in a system is a structural attitude; the use of cache memory is an organizational issue; the cache organization (e.g., direct-mapping or set-associative method) is an implementation decision; and the amount of interference in a multiprocessor system is a performance attitude.

In this text, architecture indicates the structure of a microprocessor from a programmer's point of view—i.e., number and length of registers, instruction set, and addressing modes. We call this type of architecture *program architecture*. The term *system architecture* indicates the structure of a microprocessor from a hardware perspective. We shall mention the Harvard and von Neumann architectures, providing two different structures of computer systems from a hardware perspective, but also discussing various elements of organization, such as system speed. This view is a "system" or "generic" architecture.

Interaction between a processor's program and system architectures always has had a profound influence on the cost-performance ratios attainable for the architecture.

Von Neumann Architecture vis-a-vis Harvard Architecture

The basic von Neumann architecture is shown in Fig. 1–2.

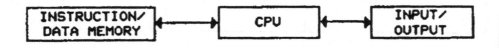

Fig. 1-2. The von Neumann architecture

A von Neumann-type computer is divided into two main

modules — i.e., the control unit and the data unit. The control unit orchestrates the entire operation of the computer by generating the control signals that activate the particular components involved in the execution of an instruction. The data unit contains the components that are used to manipulate the operands involved in a particular instruction. For example, two operands are added in the data unit (arithmetic-logic unit) of the computer. Both the control unit and the data unit contain a number of registers.

The von Neumann architecture has served the computer industry faithfully for many years and has been enhanced considerably since its conception. It is, however, still plagued by several weaknesses. Sequential, and frequent, accessing of memory creates bottlenecking and limits the flexibility of operation. Also, the "control flow" of operation, as opposed to data flow, is regarded by some as a limitation to performance. Finally, the fact that both data and instructions must reside in the same memory reduces bandwidth. Bandwidth is the maximum number of bytes per second that a system can accept or deliver. Thus, when a designer selects an operand or data word size, the designer specifies the instruction word length as well.

In a Harvard-type architecture, shown in Fig. 1–3, instructions and data are stored in separate memory modules. Introduction of this type of architecture did not create nearly the notoriety of the von Neumann computer. In fact, the Harvard architecture remained dormant until recently, when several microprocessor manufacturers realized that performance merits can be derived from the use of separate data and instruction memories.

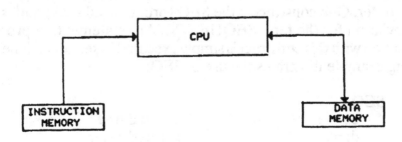

Fig. 1-3. The Harvard architecture

A significant advantage of the Harvard architecture is that, by use of separate memories, a designer provides greater flexibility in word size selection. Thus, an increase in bandwidth allows overlapping of instruction and data accesses that increase the performance. In the design of a von Neumann processor, if, for example, a designer selects a 32-bit data word size, the instruction word size must be either 32 bits or factors of 32 bits. The Harvard architecture does not impose this restriction. Thus, a Harvard-based design that uses 4-bit operands may have an instruction size of any length, for data and instructions do not reside in the same memory.

Parallel versus Multiprocessor

Several terms, such as *parallel processing, multimicroprocessing, multiprogramming,* and *multitasking,* are used to indicate the overall structure and programming capabilities of a microprocessor system. Often these terms are used interchangeably, but they are not necessarily similar. For example, a program may be divided into various tasks that can be executed concurrently by a single processor or multiple processors. A multiprocessor system, on the other hand, consists of multiple processors and some shared memory. Stated in another way, execution of concurrent processes does not necessarily require multiple processors, but, to satisfy the definition, a multiprocessor system must be equipped with n number of processors.

To explain parallel processing more clearly, we shall discuss briefly two constructs used by Occam2, the programming language of the Transputer. One construct is the SEQ (pronounced seek) and is the abbreviation for the term SEQUENCE. Any statement, or process, associated with this construct is simply executed in sequence. The following example illustrates the use of SEQ:

```
SEQ
    c := 1              Executed first
    d: = 2              Executed second
    e := c + d          Executed third
```

The SEQ construct will terminate after execution of the third process.

The PAR construct is the abbreviation for the term PARALLEL. All processes associated with a PAR construct start to execute simultaneously. For example, the processes associated with the following SEQ constructs will execute in parallel:

```
PAR
    SEQ
        IN: = 1
        d : = 2
    SEQ
        OUT: = 3
        g : = 4
```

Although the processes are shown in sequential order, they are executed in parallel. Their sequential order is a matter of writing convenience. If, for example, there are six SEQ constructs within a PAR construct, they appear rather awkward if placed alongside each other.

On the other hand, a multiprocessor system, as shown in Fig. 1–4, must consist of a number of processors and some amount of shared memory (there are several multiprocessor systems that employ memory configurations other than the shared type).

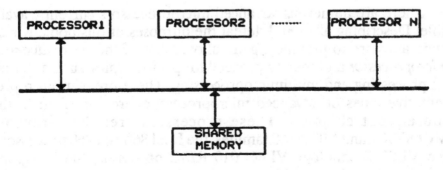

Fig. 1-4. Multiprocessor system with shared memory

Multiprogramming

The term *multiprogramming* indicates that more than one program is in some state of execution at the same time. The operating system, through its various control programs, keeps track of the amount and location of available memory and the specific memory regions allocated to programs currently in memory. As programs (tasks) are read into the computer, it stores certain information associated with the programs. The name of a program and the location where the information about the program is stored are placed on a list called the *job* (task). As memory becomes available, programs to be executed are loaded into memory in accordance with their size and arrival time. Information about these programs, such as name and location, is placed on the "ready" queue. As processing continues, programs are categorized as either active, ready, or waiting.

Topology

The term *topology* is used to indicate the interconnection strategy of a multiprocessor-based system.

There are numerous advanced microprocessors currently available. Describing all would defeat the purposes of this book, whose main aims are to provide a general overview of the term *advanced microprocessor* and then to proceed to specific topics, such as parallel processing and multimicroprocessing. Therefore, certain representative types of advanced microprocessors are described in the subsequent chapters. These processors are: the Motorola MC68XXX and MC88100 families, the Intel 860 and 960 processors, the VLSI Technology VL86C010 RISC processor, the Integraph Clipper, the Advanced Micro Devices Am29000 processor, and the Inmos Transputer. The latter processor occupies a fair portion of this book, because the processor is ideally suited to parallel applications.

Orthogonality

Orthogonality of a processor provides significant assistance to compiler designers. Orthogonality is a measure of the number and power of features implemented (the fewer and more powerful, the better) and the regularity with which groups of these features combine (the fewer special restrictions, the better). For example, the addressing modes of the MC68000 are orthogonal with respect to the address registers; there is no restriction on which address register is to be used with a given addressing mode. Consequently, all address registers are easily accessible to a compiler.

Similarly, orthogonality of instructions crossed with the addressing modes also makes selection of an addressing mode by compilers more effective.

Finally, the orthogonality of data register usage with instructions reduces restrictions on the specification of a particular data register.

Granularity

Granularity of a processor is fine if the subcomputations in the algorithm are primitive — that is, implemented by a single instruction. Granularity is coarse if the subcomputations are implemented by another algorithm.

SUMMARY

Microprocessors have come a long way, from simple 4-bit devices (4004) to extremely sophisticated processors (i860) almost equivalent in performance to a supercomputer. This significant enhancement was brought about by the increase in system clock speed, increase of bandwidth, addition of more registers, pipelining and parallelism, various memory-management techniques, and other features that have given tremendous potential to a microprocessor. At the same time, operating systems and high-level languages have been improved to maintain the same pace with the circuit enhancements. Parallel C, Parallel Fortran, Parallel Pascal, Parallel Ada are among the enhanced languages.

NOTES

[1] Michael J. Flynn, "Some Computer Organizations and Their Effectiveness," *I. E. E. E. Transactions on Computers*, C-21, No. 9 (September 1972)
[2] Jean-Loup Baer, "Computer Architecture," *Computer*, 17, No. 10 (October 1984)

Chapter 2
Advanced Computer Concepts

GENERAL COMMENTS

Designers often must address the question of which microprocessor is best suited for a particular task. To answer this question, a designer must consider, in connection with a particular microprocessor: (a) the data types that the microprocessor handles; (b) its "semantic gap"; (c) its instruction set, including its complexity or simplicity and its usefulness; and (d) its addressing modes.

DATA AND DATA TYPES

Data elements, which are implemented in a microprocessor simply as a collection of bits, can be used to represent any kind of information. Often the information to be represented is numeric, but this need not be the case. A single bit may signal the state of a digital input or output line, or a group of bits may be coded to represent text or other information.

Most programming languages provide some predefined data types, which may be used directly in a program. A data type definition can be regarded as a code that translates some kind of information into an internal representation in a microprocessor. Some languages allow users to define new data types, either by combining extant data types into new structures or by specifying the characteristics of a data type, starting anew.

Instructions of most advanced microprocessors can reference 8-

19

bit, 16-bit, 32-bit, and 64-bit operands. The i860 even references 128-bit operands. The paragraphs that follow describe the most common data types used by advanced microprocessors.

Boolean

A Boolean data type is the smallest, representing "true" or "false."

Integer

An integer data type is represented in 2s complement form. Thus, a 32-bit integer can represent a value between -2,147,483,648 to +2,147,483,647, inclusive. Normally, an arithmetic operation that involves an 8-bit or 16-bit operand in a microprocessor whose standard operand length is 32 bits is performed by sign extension of the 8-bit or 16-bit quantity and use of a 32-bit operation. For example, the operand 00001000, representing +8, will be sign-extended to 00000000000000000000000000001000. The most significant bit (leftmost bit) is the sign bit and is extended to the left by the addition of 0s up to the 32nd bit. A negative operand would be extended by the placement of 1s up to the 32nd bit.

Some microprocessors represent signed integers as INT16, INT32, or INT64, while others use the following notation:

> Quadword: 64-bit operand.
> Longword: 32-bit operand.
> Word: 16-bit operand.
> Byte: 8-bit operand.

The term *word* often is used to indicate the default data length that a microprocessor handles. That length is associated with the width of the data bus. For example, a 16-bit microprocessor will have a default data length of 16 bits, although the processor may be able to manipulate longer or shorter data.

Ordinal

An ordinal is an unsigned integer. For example, a 32-bit ordinal can represent values between 0 and 4,294,967,295.

Real Operands

A real operand, either single-precision or double-precision, is a binary floating-point number.

Figures 2–1 and 2–2 depict, respectively, the ANSI/IEEE Standard 754 formats of a single-precision real operand and a double-precision real operand.

```
Bit 31                  23                      0
-------------------------------------------------------------
  /S/     Exponent        /      Fraction        /
```

Bit 31: Sign
Bits 30–23: Exponent
Bits 22–0: Fraction

Fig. 2-1. ANSI/IEEE Standard 754 single-precision
real operand

```
Bit 63                  52                      0
-------------------------------------------------------------
  /S/     Exponent        /      Fraction        /
```

Fig. 2-2. ANSI/IEEE Standard double-precision
real operand

Literal

A literal is textual representation of a known value in accordance with some character code. For example, under the American Standard Code for Information Interchange (ASCII), the decimal value for the literal A is 65. ASCII alphanumeric and special characters (! , . # $ etc.) are represented in a microprocessor as 8-bit values.

Literals are combined to form strings. Strings usually may be broken over several lines by the placement of a "terminator" character, such as an asterisk, at the end of the broken line. Some microprocessors require a similar character at the starting point of the continuation line.

Pixels

Some microprocessors that have been designed for use in graphics applications handle the data type pixel. The Intel i860 is such a microprocessor.

A pixel may be 8, 16, or 32 bits long, depending on color and resolution requirements.

Arrays and Records

The data types described so far are called *primitive*. Naturally, any type of single data item has insignificant use in real applications, because the datum required to describe anything in the real world usually is much more complex. Consequently, it is advantageous to group single data into data structures.

A simple construct that can be used in a variety of combinations to represent data structures of any complexity is called an *array*. Arrays are used frequently in high-level languages.

Another type of data structure used in high-level languages is the record. A record enables data items associated in some way to be grouped and referred to by a single name. A record is simply a collection of (probably dissimilar) data types.

SEMANTIC GAP

Each microprocessor has a "semantic gap," which is the conceptual gap between program architecture and system architecture. Most designers attempt to reduce this gap.

INSTRUCTION SETS

According to Flynn et al. [1], an instruction is a specification of logical entities consisting of a format, an operation, a number of source operands, a result operand, and a next instruction location. A computer's instruction set is the set of all instructions that can be executed.

The past decade has seen the emergence of two schools of thought on the instruction set of a digital computer. The older school claims that a digital computer must be rich in instructions, both complex and simple. The newer school promotes the idea of a reduced-instruction-set computer (RISC).

RISC proponents have actively attempted to cement their design ideas, and most manufacturers have produced advanced microprocessors based on the RISC philosophy. According to R. Colwell et al. [2], however, the RISC publicity has "swept away objectivity in the technical communities and obscured many important issues. RISC design seriously challenges some implicit assumptions that have guided computer design for years. A study of its principles should yield a deeper understanding of hardware/software tradeoffs, computer performance, the influence of VLSI on processor design, and many other topics."

Most currently available advanced microprocessors have long instructions (most are 32 bits, although there are shorter instructions). The addressing modes of such microprocessors also have become more complex; register addressing is used extensively. In the design of both the instruction set and the addressing modes of advanced microprocessors, emphasis has been placed on high-level language support.

ADDRESSING MODES

The addressing modes outlined in this section are neither unique nor the only addressing modes available in advanced microprocessors. To make the description of addressing modes more realistic, a currently available microprocessor family, the Motorola 68000, is used. Its modes are typical.

Table 2–1 lists the various addressing modes of the 68000 family of microprocessors.

An effective address is an address that contains an operand and is part of the operation word. This address consists of two 3-bit subfields — i.e., the mode and the register. The mode bits define the addressing mode of an instruction, and the register bits designate the register involved (0 through 7). For absolute and immediate addressing, the mode bits remain the same (111), while the register bits contain a code that, in absolute addressing, distinguishes between long and short and, in immediate addressing, denotes that particular mode. The various effective address combinations are shown in Table 2–2.

As shown in Fig. 2–3, to specify an operand completely, an effective address may need additional information, ranging in length from one to several words. That is, depending on the addressing mode selected, additional 16-bit extension words may follow the opcode. The words provide additional addressing information and may extend the total length of an instruction by as much as 10 bytes.

The MC68000 manipulates single effective-address or double effective-address instructions. In a single effective-address, as shown in Fig. 2–4, the 16-bit operand word contains the opcode, the data size, and the 6-bit effective address.

Table 2-1. Addressing modes of the 68000 family

Register Direct Addressing
Data register direct $EA = D_n$
Address register direct $EA = A_n$
Status register direct $EA = SR$

Absolute Direct Addressing
Absolute short $EA = (next\ word)$
Absolute long $EA = (next\ two\ words)$

Program Counter Relative Addressing
Relative with offset $EA = (PC) + d_{16}$
Relative with index and offset $EA = (PC) + (X_n) + d_8$

Register Indirect Addressing
Register indirect $EA = A_n$
Postincrement register indirect $EA = A_n$
                                             $A < {---} A_n + N$
Predecrement register indirect $A < {---} A_n - N$
                                             $EA = (A_n)$
Register indirect with offset $EA = (A_n) + d_{16}$
Indexed register indirect with offset $EA = (A_n) + (X_n) + d_8$

Immediate Addressing
Immediate   Data = Next word or words
Quick immediate   Inherent data

Implied Addressing
Implied register $EA = SR, USP, SP, PC$

KEY:
A_n, D_n: Address register and data register, respectively, with subscript
to denote number of register
d_n: Displacement, with subscript to denote number of bits
EA: Effective address
N: Value ($N = 1, 2,$ or 4)
PC: Program counter
SP: System stack pointer
SR: Status register
USP: User stack pointer
X_n: Address or data register used as index register
$()$: Contents of

EA MODE	REGISTER	ADDRESSING MODE	NOTATION
		Table 2-2. Effective-address combinations	
000	#	Data register direct	D_n
001	#	Address register direct	A_n
010	#	Address register indirect	(A_n)
011	#	Address register indirect with postincrement	$(A_n)+$
100	#	Address register indirect with predecrement	$-(A_n)$
101	#	Address register indirect with displacement	$d(A_n)$
110	#	Address register indirect with index	$d(A_n, R_x)$
111	000	Absolute short	$XXXX
111	001	Absolute long	$XXXXXXXX
111	100	Immediate	#XXXX

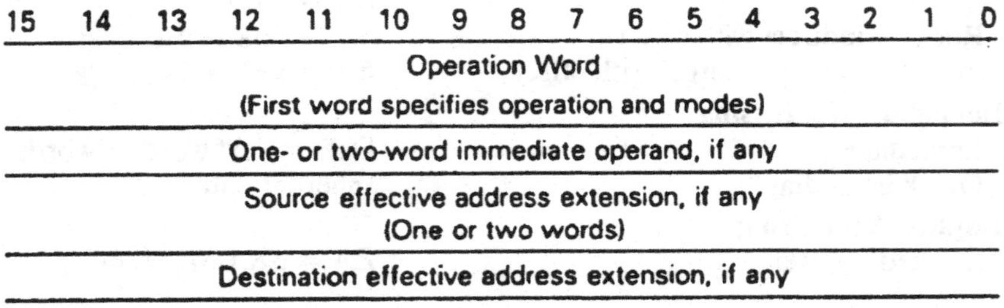

15	14	13	12	11	10	9	8	7	6	5	4	3	2	1	0

Operation Word
(First word specifies operation and modes)

One- or two-word immediate operand, if any

Source effective address extension, if any
(One or two words)

Destination effective address extension, if any

Fig. 2-3. Operand specification as performed by the 68000

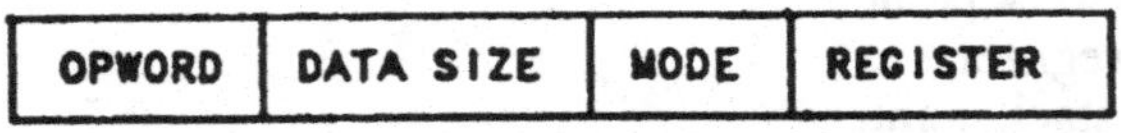

OPWORD	DATA SIZE	MODE	REGISTER

Fig. 2-4. Single effective-address instruction

Register Direct Modes

In two of the register direct modes, an operand is held in either a data register or an address register.

Notations: An   Address Register n
                   Dn   Data Register n
where n is the register number (0 to 7).

Examples:

CLR.L   D0   Clear all 32 bits of data register 0.

ADD   A1,A2   Add low-order word of address register 1 to low-order word of address register 2.

Data registers can manipulate 8-bit, 16-bit, and 32-bit operands. Address registers can manipulate 16-bit and 32-bit operands.

Memory Address Modes

General. A memory address mode is used to access an operand in a memory location. All modes in this category are variations of indirect addressing and can be used as reference pointers to memory to process sequential data, to perform stacking operations, to move blocks of data, and to manipulate elements within an array.

Address Register Indirect. This mode can be used as a variable reference pointer to memory. The address of the operand is held in an address register specified in the effective address register subfield.

Notation: (An)   (The parentheses denote "contents of")

Examples:

    MOVE   #5,(A5)   Move the value 5 to the word located at the address contained in A5.

    SUB.L   (A1),D0   Subtract from D0 the value in the longword located at the address contained in A1.

Address Register Indirect with Postincrement. In this mode, the address of an operand is held in an address register specified in the effective-address register subfield. After the address has been used, it is incremented by 1, 2, or 4, depending on whether the accessed operand is a byte, word, or longword. If, however, the address register is the stack pointer and the operand is a byte, the address is incremented by 2, in order to keep the stack pointer on a word boundary (an even address).

    This mode is useful for handling sequential data, such as tables, for moving blocks of data, and for stack unloading operations.

    Notation: (An)+

Examples:

    MOVE.B   (A2)+,D2   Move byte whose address is in A2 to low-order byte of D2; increment A2 by 1.

    MOVE.L   (A4)+,D3   Move longword whose address is in A4 to D3; increment A4 by 4.

Address Register Indirect with Predecrement. This mode works in a manner opposite to the address register indirect with postincrement; that is, this mode decrements an address before use. Therefore, this mode is suitable for stack loading operations (first-in, first-out) and also for processing of sequential data in a descending order.

Notation: -(An)

Examples:

CLR	-(A2)	Subtract 2 from A2; clear word whose address is now in A2.
CMP.L	-(A0),D0	Subtract 4 from A0; compare longword whose address is now in A0 with contents of D0.

Address Register Indirect with Displacement. When this mode is used, the address of the operand is the sum of the address held in an address register and a sign-extended, 16-bit displacement.

This addressing mode is suitable for accessing elements within an array or for accessing input-output locations within a memory range assigned to input-output devices. Use of positive or negative displacement values allows accessing of locations ahead of or behind a base address.

The address register indirect with displacement mode also is suitable for accessing individual variables in the stack. For example, one area in the stack may be used to store local variables, while another area stores data passed to subroutines. With the positive-negative displacement technique, the two stack areas may be accessed at will.

Notation: d(An)

Examples:

AVAL	EQU 5	The pseudoinstruction EQU

		assigns the value of 5 to the label AVAL.
CLR.B	AVAL(A0)	Clear byte whose address is given by adding the value of AVAL to the contents of A0.
MOVE	#2,10(A2)	Move value 2 to the word whose address is given by adding 10 to the contents of A2.

Address Register Indirect with Index and Displacement. In this mode, the address of the operand is the sum of the address held in an address register; the sign-extended, low-order, 8-bit displacement; and the contents of an index register. The latter can be either a data register or an address register.

Notations:	d(An,Ri) d(An,Ri.W)	Specify low-order word of index register
	d(An,Ri.L)	Specifies entire contents of index register.

Examples:

ADD	AVAL(A1,D2),D5	Add to the low-order word of D5 the word whose address is given by addition of the contents of A1, the low-order word of index register D2, and the displacement of AVAL.
MOVE	D5,$20(A2,A3.L)	Move entire contents of D5 to the longword whose address is given by addition of

the contents of A2, the contents of the entire index register A3, and the displacement $20.

Special Address Modes

General. A code, rather than a register number, in the effective address designates one of three special addressing modes: absolute short, absolute long, or immediate.

Absolute Short. In this mode, an extension word holds the address of the operand. Therefore, before use, the 16-bit address is sign-extended. Thus, the absolute short mode can define a permanent address within a 64-kilobyte range.

Example:

    JMP $400

Absolute Long. Unlike the absolute short mode, which operates within the low or high 64 kilobytes of memory, the absolute long mode can be used within the entire 16-megabyte memory area. This mode requires two words of extension. These two 16-bit words are "joined" (first word: Address High; second word: Address Low) to form the address of the operand.

Example:

    JMP $12000

Immediate Mode. In the immediate mode, any value after the opcode is the operand.

Examples:

MOVE	#1,D0	Move value 1 to the low-order word of D0.

SUB.L	#1,D0	Subtract 1 from the entire contents of D0.

Program Control Modes

General. The modes in the program control category load a new address to the program counter and transfer execution of the program starting at the new address.

Program Counter with Displacement. One word extension is used in the program counter mode with displacement. The address of an operand is the sum of the contents of the program counter and a sign-extended, 16-bit displacement in the extension word. The content of the program counter is the address in the extension word.

Example:

JMP	TAG(PC)	Force the evaluation of "TAG" to be program counter-relative.

Program Counter with Index. This mode requires one word of extension. The address of an operand is the sum of the program counter contents, an 8-bit displacement (low-order byte of the extension word), and the contents of the index register.

One advantage of the program counter mode is that it can be used in the manipulation of position-independent programs. Since the program counter always contains the location of the next instruction, the current instruction may refer to data or program locations for branches relative to the instruction itself.

A restriction has been placed on this mode, and for a good reason: it cannot be used to specify a destination operand. This restriction prevents a program that contains errors from destroying itself inadvertently. The restriction also prevents programmers from using the dangerous practice of writing self-modifying code.

Examples:

MOVE	T(D2),TABLE	Move the word at location T and contents of D2 to the word location defined by TABLE. T must be a relocatable symbol.
JMP	TABLE(A2.W)	Transfer control to the location defined by TABLE and lower 16-bit content of A2 with sign extension. TABLE must be a relocatable symbol.
JMP	TAG(PC,A2.W)	Force evaluation of "TAG" to be program counter-relative with index.

Inherent Mode

The inherent mode is not classed with the others because it contains very few instructions. Inherent instructions usually do not show an operand. The operation word itself normally indicates the location of the operand.

The MC68000 family of microprocessors has been designed to facilitate multiprocessing. Some of the multiprocessing capabilities, and the instructions used for that purpose, are discussed in later chapters.

PIPELINING

General Description

Though performance of microprocessors has been increased considerably by faster clock speeds, there are still natural limitations. Pipelining is another technique used to improve the performance of a digital computer.

This technique is a form of parallel processing, since several operations on the contents of the pipeline occur simultaneously. The advantage of an instruction pipeline is in staging the activity associated with instruction execution in such a way that the time needed to decode the instruction and to provide the control for execution is not visible outside the chip. This task is accomplished by the execution of a different instruction in each of the various stages of the pipeline simultaneously.

Pipeline is a name borrowed from a physical pipeline in which, e.g., a fluid chemical undergoes various changes while flowing through the pipeline. A computer pipeline more closely resembles an industrial assembly line, as shown in Fig. 2–5.

T	TR	TRA	TRAC	TRACT	TRACTO	TRACTOR	
TTTT	RRRR	AAAA	CCCC	TTTT	OOOO	RRRR	
1st	2nd	3rd	4th	5th	6th	7th	LEVEL

(a)

IF——>ID ——>AG ——>OF——>IE ——>OS ——>UPC

(b)

CLOCK CYCLE	1	2	3	4	5	6	7	8	9
Instruction No. 1	IF	ID	AG	OF	IE	OS	UPC		
Instruction No. 2		IF	ID	AG	OF	IE	OS	UPC	
Instruction No. 3			IF	ID	AG	OF	IE	OS	UPC

(c)

Fig. 2-5. Pipelining illustrated

In Fig. 2–5a, assuming that each letter in the word "TRACTOR" represents a separate but integral component of the complete system, each stage, or level, of the assembly operation adds such a component to a tractor, until an entire tractor is complete. While the first tractor enters level 2, a second tractor enters level 1. While the first tractor enters level 3, the second tractor enters level 2, and a new tractor enters level 1, and so on.

The representation in Fig. 2–5b shows the flow of an instruction through a nonpipelined computer, as a sequence of the following steps:

1. Instruction Fetch (IF): A copy of an instruction is obtained from main memory.
2. Instruction Decode (ID): The computer's control unit decodes the instruction opcode, and the necessary control signals are generated to activate the appropriate circuits in the computer involved in the execution of the particular instruction.
3. Address Generation (AG): The effective address of operands is calculated.
4. Operand Fetch (OF): The operand, if required (READ operation), is obtained from memory.
5. Instruction Execution (IE): The instruction is executed.
6. Operand Store (OS): The operand is stored (for WRITE operations).
7. Update Program Counter (UPC): The address of the next instruction is generated.

Fig. 2–5c shows the same steps; these steps are executed, however, in a pipelined environment – i.e., concurrently.

Pipelining significantly improves the throughput of a computer. Refer again to Fig. 2–5b. The time that this nonpipelined computer needs for execution of an instruction is $T_{np} = t_1 + t_2 = t_3 + t_4 + t_5 + t_6 + t_7$. The throughput of this computer is $1/T_{np}$. Assume, in the case of Fig. 2–5c, that $t_b = \max\{t_1, t_2, ...\}$ = speed of the slowest point in the pipeline. Then the throughput for the pipelined computer is $1/t_b$, and that is the maximum throughput of the pipelined computer, because, for every $T_p = t_b$ units of time, and assuming that instructions are independent, an instruction can leave the pipeline after its execution [3]. It can be shown that $T_p = T_{np}$, indicating that the throughput of a pipelined computer can be much higher than that of a nonpipelined computer. The slowest point of the pipeline determines this throughput. In Fig. 2–5c, it is assumed that every step of an instruction requires one clock cycle for completion. Consider, however, the case of Fig. 2–6a, in which step 2 of the instruction requires three time units for completion and, thus, is the slowest point of execution.

Figures 2–6b and 2–6c show two techniques that can improve this "bottlenecking." In Fig. 2–6b, the slowest part has been subdivided into three separate subparts, while, in Fig. 2–6c, it has been arranged in parallel. This latter technique creates problems in distribution and synchronization of the tasks in the pipeline.

STEP 1	STEP 2	STEP 3		
1t	3t	1t		

> time

(a)

STEP 1	STEP 2a	STEP 2b	STEP 2c	STEP 3
1t	1t	1t	1t	1t

> time

(b)

STEP 1	STEP 2	STEP 3
	STEP 2 3t	
1t	STEP 2 3t	STEP 3 1t
1t	STEP 2	

(c)

Fig. 2-6. Bottlenecking improvement

In Fig. 2–6c, the first instruction that could use an operand that instruction 1 loads is instruction 3. If instruction 2 needs to use the same operand, a "wait-state" would have to be introduced into the pipeline. Since at least one instruction must be located between a LOAD instruction and the first instruction that uses the loaded operand, there is a "load latency" and, in this case, it is one clock period. A load latency is a nightmare for a designer of a reduced-instruction-set computer.

Figure 2–5b demonstrates that, in a nonpipelined computer, an instruction follows a certain sequence of steps from the time that the instruction is fetched from memory until it is executed. The procedure is different in a pipeline. As the steps for completion of, say, instructions $i + 1, i + 2,...i + n$ are overlapped, these instructions may be fetched and executed before instruction i is completed. This ability creates what is called a *pipeline timing hazard*, because instructions $i + 1,...i + n$ may require the result of instruction i while it cannot be provided. This type of dependency must be considered seriously during the design stage of a pipeline, and circuits, called *interlocks*, must be included to detect and to resolve a timing hazard.

The depth of the pipeline is an idealized performance multiplier. Several factors prevent achievement of this increase. First, delays are introduced whenever data needed to execute an instruction is still in the pipeline. Second, pipelines break because of branches (described in a subsequent paragraph). Third, the complexity of managing the pipeline and handling breaks adds overhead to the basic logic and, thus, degrades the rate at which the pipeline levels can complete their task.

Referring again to Fig. 2–5c, that particular pipeline has a latency of six clock cycles. When the branch is completed, the results of some instructions must be discarded; this is an inefficient way of performing a branch.

Reduction of Pipeline Latency

The effects of pipeline latency may be reduced by careful design methods in the selection of the pipeline structure and the way in which branching is carried out.

Optimizing Compiler. Use of an optimizing compiler is one of the ways to minimize branch latency.

An optimizing compiler rearranges the generated code of a program by minimizing its size and execution time. The optimization occurs after the initial phases of code generation have been completed. The optimizer inspects large portions of the compiled program for frequently recurring cases in which the compiled results can be improved.

The following five operations are typical of compiler optimization.

First, rather than recalculate a produced result, an optimizing compiler may reuse the result. A calculation is carried out once, and the compiler saves the result for later use. Redundant recalculations are not apparent in the source code but are created by the underlying definitions of high-level operations.

Second, a compiler may reduce the amount of code execution within a loop. More often than not, only a few computations change on different loop iterations. The optimizing compiler attempts to reduce to a minimum the amount of work that is performed within loops by moving loop-invariant computations outside the loops.

The third operation involves replacement of slow operations by faster ones. For example, some special cases of multiplication and division can be replaced by faster shift and add instructions. As the slow operations are most general, they are generated during the first phases of compilation, and the early code-generation phases cannot recognize those special cases that allow the operations to be replaced with faster ones.

Fourth is allocation of processor registers so that they contain frequently used data, which reduces the number of frequent memory accesses by replacement with faster, register accesses.

The fifth typical operation involves scheduling the execution of instructions optimally. The optimizing compiler attempts to move instructions to a point in the program flow where those instructions create fewer problems for the processor's pipeline. For example, the instruction to load a register may be moved to a point in the instruction sequence where the memory reference of the instruction can be overlapped with other instructions.

Most optimizations rely on two types of information: one about program flow and the other on data dependencies that the program flow creates. Optimization is achieved not because the optimizing compiler comprehends the task being executed, but because it comprehends the dependencies embedded in the generated code. Thus, the optimizing compiler rearranges the instruction sequence so that any dependencies are minimized.

Delayed Branching. Delayed branching, to reduce pipeline penalties associated with changes in program flow, is another added feature of advanced microprocessors.

At this point, a distinction must be made between the terms *pipeline* and *instruction queue*. When a change in instruction flow occurs — e.g., a branch — the instruction pipeline must be filled before the new instruction can be executed. The instruction queue, on the other hand, needs only the first word present. During execution of in-line code, however, an instruction queue does not provide the performance benefits of a pipeline. Instruction queues tend to saturate the bus with instruction fetches that are discarded after a change-of-flow instruction. When one considers that a change-of-flow instruction occurs 25 to 30% of the time and that instruction accesses that may be discarded can prevent necessary data accesses, the advantage of an instruction pipeline is evident.

Depth

A good example of a pipeline is found in the Motorola 68020, whose instruction pipeline has a depth of three words, as shown in Fig. 2–7.

Motorola increased the depth on the 68020 from two to three words because it was observed that, on a 32-bit bus, there is no performance penalty for the third element during a change-of-flow instruction. This observation is true for it is always possible to fetch three words in two accesses. Due to the possibility of branching to an odd-word address, in which case two accesses are required to fetch either two or three words, the minimum number of accesses required to branch is two.

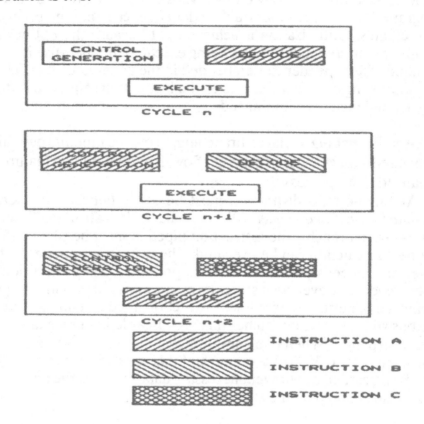

Fig. 2-7. Instruction pipeline of the Motorola 68020

A demonstration of the stubborn consistency of this principle is provided in Fig. 2–8, in which the block diagram depicts two memory configurations for the instruction stream A,B,C,D,E. If a branch to the first example (even aligned) is carried out, only one access is required to fetch two words. In the other case (odd-aligned), however, two accesses must occur to fetch the first two words. Once it is determined that two accesses are required to fill the pipeline, it can be observed that, with those two accesses, it is always possible to fetch the first three words. Thus, there is no penalty for increasing the depth of the instruction pipeline from two to three words.

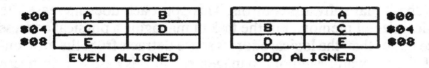

Fig. 2-8. Branch requirement of the 68020

The increase in the depth of an instruction pipeline may lead a reader to believe that this approach has only advantages and can be followed arbitrarily. There are, however, disadvantages or, at least, many situations in which the advantages are obviated, if the depth of a pipeline is not gauged correctly. It is necessary to balance the depth of a pipeline against the performance of a processor's micromachine.

Most advanced microprocessors make use of pipelining. For example, the AMD 29000 has a four-stage pipeline: fetch, decode, execute, and write-back. The pipeline is organized so that the execution rate of effective instructions may be as high as one instruction per cycle. Chapter 5 describes the 29000 in detail.

MEMORY MANAGEMENT

General Design Considerations

Direct addressing of only 64 kilobytes of memory is one of the numerous limitations that 8-bit microprocessors display. This limitation becomes more evident with today's sophisticated disk operating systems (OS/2 requires approximately two megabytes of memory) and other complex programs, such as graphics and spreadsheets.

Techniques have been devised to increase the size of an 8-bit microprocessor's physical memory. One such technique is bank switching, where a microprocessor's physical memory is divided into separate banks of memory, but each bank shares the same logical address area. Selection of a particular bank is accomplished by "switches" that software controls. This approach does increase the physical size of memory, but the task of managing a physical address space larger than the logical address space detracts from the efficiency of the software. Memory management in this case is a software overhead.

The memory limitation problem was partially corrected with the advent of newer microprocessors with wider (16-bit and 32- bit) address buses.

Another important requirement in a system is resource protection, which refers to protection of an operating system from corruption.

Furthermore, a programmer must be able to protect selected areas of code while maintaining the ability to communicate and to share other areas of code.

It is also advantageous for a system to have the capability of allocating priorities within a user address space so that a hierarchy may be built within a task, allowing restricted access to certain areas of code, under the control of an operating system.

This general description of problems and requirements encountered in the design of a microprocessor-based system can be classified under the general title of *memory management*. Advanced microprocessors are equipped, either internally or through external devices connected between a processor and the memory modules, with memory-management capabilities that control accesses, carry out mapping of addresses and, in general, behave as a routing means between the physical and logical address ranges of a microprocessor.

Segmentation

Earlier advanced microprocessors, such as the Intel 80X86 family, display segmentation, in which memory is divided into segments. For example, in the 8086, programs "view" the one megabyte of memory space that the processor is able to address directly as a group of segments defined by a particular application.

Each segment in the 8086 is a logical unit of memory that can have a maximum size of 64K. A segment consists of contiguous memory locations and is an independent, separately addressable unit. Software assigns to every segment a base address, which is the starting location of the segment in the memory space. All segments begin on 16-byte memory boundaries.

The four segments of the 8086 are: data segment, code segment, stack segment, and extra segment. A corresponding segment register, which holds a base address value, points to each segment. Programs obtain access to code and data in other segments by changing the segment registers to point to the desired segments.

To examine briefly how segmentation works, we shall again use the 8086 as an example.

It is useful to think of every memory location as consisting of two types of addresses, a physical address and a logical address. The address bus of a processor identifies the physical address. Programs, however, deal with logical rather than physical addresses; that is, a programmer does not need to know where a program is to reside in the physical memory space. This facilitates dynamic management of memory resources.

The difference between logical and physical addresses is depicted in Fig. 2–9. A logical address is composed of a segment base value, contained in a segment register, and an offset value that is part of the instruction. Thus, the segment base value could be thought of as the starting address of the particular segment, while the offset value is the "distance" between the segment base address and the desired physical address.

Figure 2–10 shows how the 8086 generates a physical address. The processor shifts the segment base value four bit positions and adds the offset. This type of addition enables the 8086 to accomplish modulo 64K addressing, in which addresses wrap around from the end of a segment to the beginning of the same segment.

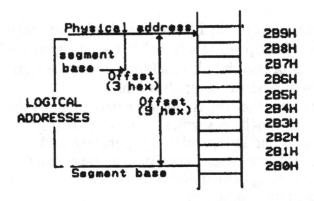

Fig. 2-9. Logical and physical addresses

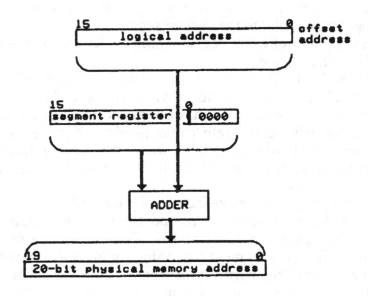

Fig. 2-10. Generation of physical address

Thus, a segmented addressing scheme allows a program to be position-independent or dynamically relocatable. The latter term allows a multiprogramming or multitasking system to make particularly effective use of available memory. Inactive programs usually are removed from memory and placed into disk storage, and the freed memory is allocated to other programs. Furthermore, if a large program needs additional memory space and such space is available only in noncontiguous segments, then other program segments can be compacted to free a contiguous space. See Fig. 2–11. See also the description of paging in the next section.

MEMORY

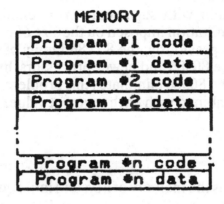

Fig. 2-11. Contiguous memory segments

Segmentation is not without problems. When segments are of different size and are swapped in and out, areas of valuable memory may become unusable, because they may be contained in between already allocated segments and may not be large enough to hold the segment that needs to be loaded. This problem is called *external fragmentation*.

Currently available memory-management devices use a powerful method, known as *binary body system*, to overcome external fragmentation.

In this method, a list of memory segments and their respective sizes is kept in memory. When a new segment is requested, a search is made to determine the availability of a segment of appropriate size. If no suitable segment is found, this method searches for an available segment of the next largest size, which, if available, is split into two pieces, called *buddies*. One piece is assigned to the request, while the other goes to the available list. If the search fails to find a suitable segment, the process may continue until the largest segment is found and split into multiple pieces, or the requesting task may be placed in a queue to await the availability of an approriate segment. Whenever the task finally releases the memory segment, it is returned to memory and, if its former buddy is still available, both pieces are recombined.

Another problem with segmentation as employed by certain processors is the limitation imposed on the size of each segment. For example, as stated previously, the 80X86 family of processors, with the exception of the 80386 and newer processors, limits the size of a segment to 64K. The 80386 eliminates this problem by allowing a 32-bit offset to be combined with each segment value.

Paging

This method divides the memory of a system into equal-sized "pages" and, thus, avoids the problem of external fragmentation. Since all pages are the same length, a newly requested page always fits into the memory space of an old, removed page.

Figure 2–12 illustrates the principle of a paging system. A set of page registers intercepts certain address bits from the processor and translates these bits to a different value via a lookup table. Consequently, the entire memory spectrum of the system is remapped as desired. In the example shown in Fig. 2–12, address bits 0 through 12 are transferred to the memory modules; thus, these bits determine the size of each page (same for all the pages, 8K). Bits 13 through 15 indicate the number of a page, 0 through 7.

Operating systems can use paging schemes to extend the addressing range of a processor and also to remap the address space. For example, 16 address bits, which normally would access only 64K of memory directly, can be expanded to 24 address bits with 256 16-bit page registers. Bits 16 through 23 of the logical address are transferred to the page register array. The content of each 16-bit page

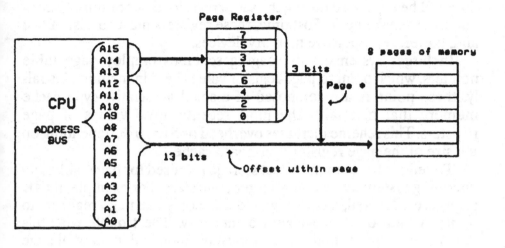

Fig. 2-12. Example of a paging scheme

register is combined with the upper 8 bits of the logical address to form a 24-bit physical address.

Paging also has problems, such as internal fragmentation. Normally, when a program needs a memory segment larger than the size of the page, two pages are allocated to accommodate the program. While the space of one page will be occupied totally, some and possibly a large amount of the space of the second page will be unused. For an optimum system, care should be taken in deciding page size, and consideration given to competing aspects, such as the overhead for generating and servicing extra page faults if small pages are used as opposed to the possibility of wasted space in the form of internal fragmentation for larger pages.

Another problem with paging is the time consumed in the manipulation of the page registers. In the example that employs a 24-bit address scheme with pages of 256 bytes each, the page registers must occupy 128 kilobytes of memory. This scheme implies not one but two problems. First, an operating system must save and reload the page registers every time the processor takes on a different process.

With the presence of 128 kilobytes of page registers, considerable time will be expended during the save and reload operations. Consequently, to make up for lost time, these registers must consist of fast and, therefore, expensive memory devices.

In larger systems, most paging schemes employ page table pointers, which point to page register values held in memory. Usually, these pointers are composed of a small associative-type cache memory that maintains the most recently used values of page registers. This scheme increases overhead by 5 to 10%, depending on the size of the page register's on-board cache.

To reduce the amount of fast storage required for page tables, an operating system may employ larger page sizes. For example, if 64K pages are allocated, a system would need only 256 page registers to remap a total of 16 megabytes of memory. The trouble with this scheme, however, is that memory must be allocated in integral page sizes, and a program that requires a full page and only a small amount of a second page leads to waste of memory space, as described previously. Furthermore, an increase in the size of pages decreases the number of page registers.

Cache Memory

Cache memory is more than a compromise between expensive memory and slow memory. Cache memory offers such substantial advantages in speed and cost that semiconductor manufacturers offer cache-memory control both as an on-chip feature and in the form of an external cache-memory controller.

Whenever a speed mismatch between main memory and a processor exists, as is almost always the case, a cache-memory circuit provides interface to take advantage of both a fast processor and the availability of slow dynamic random-access memory. The cache memory extracts from main memory and stores temporarily an amount of data adequate to satisfy a processor's requirements. Data are accessed from main memory at a slow speed but read by a processor at its high speed. As the word *cache* implies, operation of the memory is transparent to a user.

A cache-memory system functions properly because usually it can predict successfully the words that a program will require soon. If programs accessed words from memory completely at random, it would be impossible to predict the words most likely to be needed next, and a cache-memory system would perform no better than a conventional mixed memory system with a small amount of bipolar memory.

Fortunately, programs do not generate random addresses. Instead, programs have a tendency to make most accesses in the neighborhood of locations accessed in the recent past. This tendency is the basis of the principle of program locality. The fact that programs display this type of behavior makes cache-memory systems possible.

An understanding of the principle of program locality may be obtained by examining the small-scale behavior of typical data structures. Code execution generally proceeds in straight lines or loops; the next few accesses most likely will be within a few words ahead of or behind a recently accessed location. Stacks grow and shrink from one end, with the next few accesses near the current loop. Character strings and vectors often are scanned through sequentially.

The principle of program locality is a statement of how most programs tend to behave, not a law obeyed by all programs. Jumps in code sequences, seemingly random accesses of symbol tables by assemblers, and context switches between programs are examples of behavior that can affect adversely the locality of addresses that a processor generates. Never can the process of guessing the words that a program will reference next be completely successful. The percentage of correct guesses is a statistical measure affected by the size and organization of the cache, the algorithms that the cache uses, and the behavior of a program driving the cache.

There are five cache schemes, as described below.

Block Fetch. The principle of program locality dictates that, for a cache to have the best chance of containing the word that a program needs next, the cache should contain words near those accessed recently. The basic method for accomplishing this task is called *block* *fetch.* When the cache controller circuit deems it necessary to move a word of data from slow memory to fast memory, the controller will move not just the single word but a block of several adjacent words.

A block fetch scheme may provide either look-behind or look-ahead, or both, depending on the position of the originally requested word within a block. Since many important generated address sequences — e.g., most code — tend to move in ascending order, the originally requested word usually is the first in the block, so the block fetch scheme generally provides look-ahead.

The block size is one of the most important parameters in the design of a cache-memory system. If the block size is too small, a cache system will have insufficient look-ahead, and performance will suffer, particularly for programs that do not contain many loops. Furthermore, a small block size requires a system to store more addresses than a larger block, for the same total memory size.

On the other hand, a block that is too large may not provide room in the cache for enough blocks to allow adequate look-behind. Large blocks also tend to mean more memories operating in parallel within the slow memory, resulting in wider buses between slow and fast memory and, consequently, in increased cost. As a block becomes larger, each additional word in the block is less likely to be useful, since the word is farther from the originally requested word and less likely to be needed soon by a program. Empirically, a block size of two words increases memory system performance dramatically, while larger block sizes result in much smaller improvements, seldom worth implementing.

Fully Associative Cache. If a cache-memory system were designed so that the fast memory held a contiguous block of, say, 1000 words, the system would be doomed to failure. Most programs make reference to code segments, subroutines, stacks, lists, and buffers located in scattered parts of the entire address spectrum.

Ideally, a 1000-word cache would hold those 1000 words that the controller circuit considered most likely to be required, no matter how scattered throughout the address space of main memory those words were. Since no relation would exist among all of the addresses of these 1000 words to each other or to any single register or mapping function, each word in the fast memory would have to carry its address with it. Then, when the processor requested a word from memory, the cache simply would compare (associate) the address from the processor with each of the 1000 addresses of words in the fast memory. If a match were found, the data for that address would be sent to the processor. This is the principle of an associative memory, illustrated in Fig. 2–13.

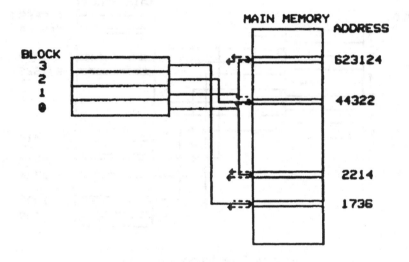

Fig. 2-13. Fully associative cache-memory system

This system, called *fully associative* because the incoming address must be compared (associated) with all of the stored addresses, provides the cache-controller circuit maximum flexibility in deciding which words the controller wants in memory—i.e., any words at all until the memory is full. Unfortunately, 1000 address comparisons would be unacceptably slow and expensive. One of the basic dilemmas of cache organization is how to provide minimum restrictions on the groups of words to be present in fast memory while limiting the required number of address comparisons.

Direct-Mapping Cache. A direct-mapping cache compares a single address. The many address comparisons of a fully associative cache are needed because any block from main memory may be placed in any block of fast memory. Thus, every block of fast memory must be checked to determine whether that block has each requested address. The direct-mapping method allows each block from main memory only one possible location in fast memory, as shown in Fig. 2–14.

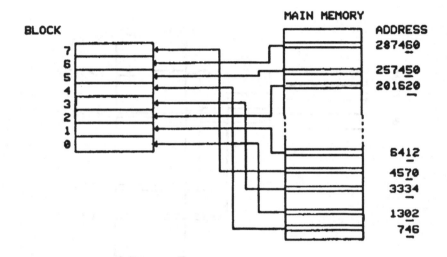

Fig. 2-14. Direct-mapping cache

Consider each incoming address as composed of three parts. The first part starts at bit 0 and contains enough bits to specify a requested byte. The next field, called the *index field*, starts where the first field ends and contains enough bits to specify a block in fast memory. The third field, called the *address field*, contains the rest of the bits.

For example, consider an 18-bit byte address as input to a 256-word, four-word-per-block, direct-mapping cache. This cache would be four words wide and 64 blocks deep. An assumption of four words per block allows us to break down an address conveniently, using octal notation. As illustrated in Fig. 2–15, the word field is composed of bits 2, 1, and 0, where bit 0 indicates the byte, and bits 2 and 1 indicate the word. The index field is composed of bits 8 through 3 and indicates the block. The address field is composed of bits 17 through 9.

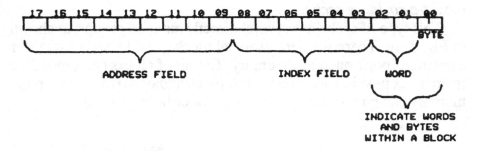

Fig. 2-15. 18-Bit byte address breakdown

If word 27435 is requested, the cache controller circuit points to the address that goes with the information currently in block 35 in fast memory. If that address is 274, the controller sends the third word in that block to the processor. If the stored address is not 274, the controller must fetch block 27435 from main memory, transmit the third word in the block to the processor, load the block into block 35 of the fast memory, replacing the previous contents in that block, and change the address field stored with block 35 to 274.

Notice also that only the address field of the address need be stored with each block, as only that field is required for comparison. The index field need not be compared because anything stored in fast memory block 35 has an index field of 35. The word field need not be compared because, if the block is present, every word in the block is present.

There are some disadvantages to the simple scheme of direct-mapping cache. If the processor in the example makes frequent references to both locations 274356 and 6352, there will be frequent references to slow memory, because only one of these locations can be in the cache at one time. Fortunately, this sort of program behavior is infrequent, so that the direct-mapping cache, although offering significantly poorer performance than the fully associative method, is adequate for some applications.

Set-Associative Cache. Usually a system of choice is a compromise between a direct-mapping cache and a fully associative cache, called the *set-associative cache.*

This type of cache has several directly mapped groups, as shown in Fig. 2–16. There is a set of several blocks, one in each group, for each index position in fast memory. The set of blocks corresponding to an index position is called a *set.* A block of data arriving from main memory can go into any group at its proper index position.

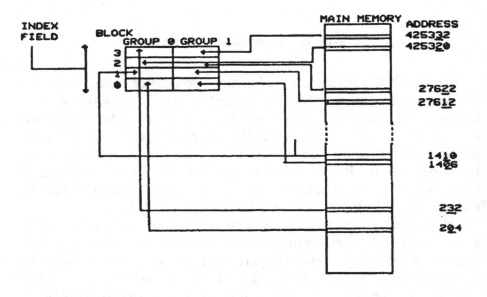

Fig. 2-16. Set-associative cache memory system

As there are several places for storage of data with the same index field in the addresses, excessive main memory traffic, while possible, is less likely to occur. This facet of a set-associative cache provides higher performance. In fact, a four-way set-associative cache (four groups) normally will perform very nearly as well as a fully associative cache.

The price to be paid for higher performance is some increase in complexity. There are several places in fast memory where any given piece of data can be stored, so the controller must do several comparisons — i.e., associations — to determine the location of requested data. The number of times that the controller must compare is of course equal to the number of groups, usually two, three, or four. A set-associative cache can be classified as an n-way set-associative cache, where n is the number of comparisons performed — i.e., the number of groups.

Another aspect of the increased complexity becomes apparent when a block of fast memory must be overwritten. There are now several locations in fast memory where the new data from main memory may be written (one in each group), so the controller must have some means by which to identify the block to be overwritten. The decision could be made on the basis of:

1. Least Recently Used (LRU) — the block least recently used is replaced;
2. First-in-First-Out (FIFO) — the block stored the longest is replaced; or
3. Random — blocks are replaced in a random manner.

A replacement strategy based on LRU or FIFO information requires the storage of LRU or FIFO bits, along with the address fields in the address memory, and the logic necessary to generate and decode these bits. The random strategy is far easier and cheaper to implement and yet its performance is only slightly lower than that obtainable with the other strategies.

In all but low-performance applications, the added performance of a set-associative cache usually justifies the slightly greater complexity of at least two-way associativity.

Write-Through and Write-Back Cache. Assume that the following sequence of events occurs. First, a processor accesses location 200, and the block containing this address is copied into fast memory.

Then the processor writes new data into location 200, updating this location in fast memory. Next, the processor does a reference that causes the cache controller to overwrite the block in fast memory containing location 200. If the processor again accesses location 200, the obsolete data in main memory will be loaded into fast memory — an unacceptable result. Two methods have been devised to deal with this problem. These methods are called write-through and write-back.

With write-through, whenever a write reference occurs, the data are not only stored in fast memory but also are copied immediately into main memory. These actions mean that the main memory always contains a valid copy of all data. A controller that is scheduled to overwrite a block in fast memory can do so immediately, without the loss of any data.

The advantage of write-through is that, despite its relative simplicity, the main memory always has correct data. The primary disadvantage is some reduction in speed due to the need to access the slow memory on every write reference. This disadvantage is offset somewhat by the fact that write references are a small fraction of all references to memory. In addition, the cache does not have to wait for the main memory to finish before starting the next cycle. Since a reasonable design would cycle only the memory being written into and not all of the parallel memories in main memory, even multiple sequential writes should not hold up a system. However, during some fraction of time, the system will have a read-miss following a write or two writes to the same memory stack within main memory, and then the system must wait. This wait causes a system to run slightly slower than first-order estimates would indicate.

With the other method of handling the stale data problem in a cache system, called *write-back*, data that a processor writes is stored only in the fast memory, leaving the main memory unaltered and obsolete. A bit in the address field of the block in fast memory, called the *altered bit*, is set to indicate that this block contains new information. When the controller is scheduled to overwrite a block of fast memory, the altered bit is inspected first. If this bit is set, the controller must write the block into main memory before overwriting it.

The primary advantage of write-back is higher performance. For almost any program, the number of times an altered block must be copied into main memory is smaller th~~n the number of write references, so write-back is noticeably faster than write-through. One disadvantage of write-back is increased complexity. To do double cycles, a write-back system must be capable of regenerating addresses from tags and from the additional sequencing logic.

Another disadvantage of write-back is the possible effect of a power failure. When power fails, fast memory will be holding the only valid copies of some arbitrary set of locations. Unless they are copied into main memory, they will be lost. As there is no way to know which locations have been lost, the entire memory must be considered volatile. If main memory is volatile anyway, there is no problem. Otherwise, there is, and several corrective steps must be taken.

One step is to require the power fail program to do a sequence of reads calculated to ensure that every block in the cache has been overwritten. A more reliable, but more expensive, system would ensure automatically that all altered blocks are copied into main memory, after the program halts but before power disappears.

Virtual Memory

The price of semiconductor memory has become very approachable, although its users sometimes see peaks or valleys in pricing. Nevertheless, it still is rather uneconomical to have a large amount of main memory. It is much cheaper to employ disk storage, and to apply the principle of virtual memory.

In a virtual memory system, the logical addresses that a processor issues are mapped to an auxiliary storage device, such as a hard disk, so that a user "imagines" that all of the logical addresses have been implemented. In this case, logical addresses also are called *virtual addresses*.

Naturally, significant loss of speed is a problem presented in a system that involves access to a hard disk every time a memory access must be accomplished. Therefore, some of the hard disk storage locations are still mapped to RAM, as shown in Fig. 2–17.

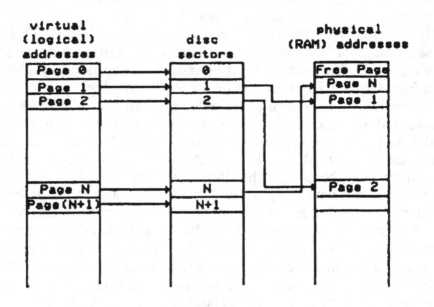

Fig. 2-17. Principle of virtual memory

In general, a computer program contains and manipulates much information — e.g., instructions, constants, work areas, and tables — but uses only a portion of that information at a time. If main memory cannot store the entire program, the program still can be executed because, at any given time, only the relevant portion need be present in main memory.

Imagine a virtual storage of some arbitrary size, such as 16 megabytes. For the incoming programs, assign to each consecutive byte a unique address, and partition this required storage into 4K bytes, called *pages*. Then subdivide the real memory into 4K byte blocks called *frames*, and partition the auxiliary storage device into 4K byte "slots." Transfer between real memory and disk then will occur in 4K byte blocks.

A two-level reference to the pages will be used. A given program occupies contiguous segments of virtual memory that contain one or more pages, as Fig. 2–18 demonstrates. Specification of the segment number, the page number within that segment, and the displacement within the page locates a given program element in virtual storage.

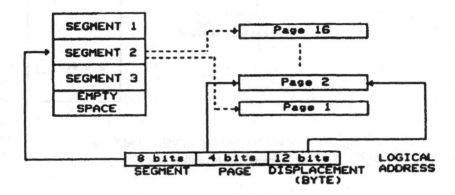

Fig. 2-18. A more detailed illustration of Fig. 2-17

The hardware circuit used to link logical addresses to the physical address that a processor needs is called the *dynamic-address-translation facility* and, also, a hard disk controller. This circuit intercepts the virtual memory addresses that a processor has assigned to a program and translates the addresses into physical addresses, as shown in Fig. 2–19. The circuit maps the example 16 megabytes of virtual memory into the smaller domain of RAM. Mapping maintenance is accomplished by a control program.

Physical addresses that the execution unit of a processor requires are derived from a program's logical, or virtual, addresses through the disk controller translator.

For a dynamic address translation, the control program maintains a segment table and associated page tables, as depicted in Fig. 2–20. The control program also stores the location of the segment table in a special table-origin register. Each entry in the segment table specifies the location in main memory for the corresponding page table. Each page table entry shows the address of the main memory

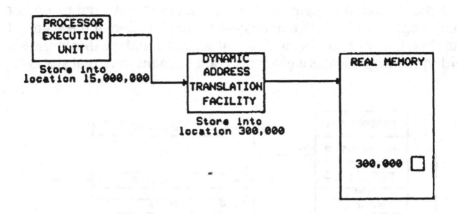

Fig. 2-19. Virtual-memory-to-physical-memory
address translation

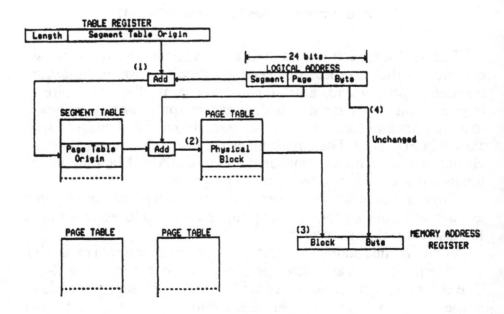

Fig. 2-20. Translation of a logical address
to a physical address

frame containing the virtual page or indicates that the page is contained in a peripheral slot. The tables reside in main memory during the execution of a program.

Briefly, the steps taken for the translation are:

1. Addition of the segment number of a logical address to the segment table origin locates the origin of the page table corresponding to the segment number;
2. Addition of the page table origin to the page number of the logical address provides the location of the page table entry with the physical block location in main memory, if present; and
3. The block location and the byte number (4) complete the memory address to be accessed by a processor.

Note that a program under execution neither knows nor needs to know where a particular virtual page is at any given time. A virtual page may be located in a frame of main memory or in the slot of a hard disk. When the required virtual page is located on a disk, its page-table entry will be flagged to generate in the processor an exception condition, which tells the control program to find a main memory storage frame for the virtual page. Then the control program initiates an i/o operation to transfer the page from the disk (page-in) and updates the page table accordingly.

If the amount of virtual storage that a program uses exceeds main memory storage, the control program must make frames available by selecting certain frames and writing the pages for those frames in i/o equipment storage slots. Once the pages have been copied out, the frames can be reused, to contain other pages. Transfer of pages from frames to slots is called *page-out*.

SUMMARY

This chapter covers new features found in currently available advanced microprocessors. Large word sizes, increased instruction sets, and more complex addressing modes, all facilitating use of high-level languages, are present. Pipelining and other forms of concurrency have increased the execution speed of microprocessors. Memory-management techniques, such as paging, segmentation, cache, and virtual memory, also are extensively used new features.

NOTES

[1] Michael J. Flynn, John D. Johnson, and Scott P. Wakefield, "On Instruction Sets and Their Formats," *I.E.E.E. Transactions on Computers*, C-34, No. 3 (March 1985)

[2] Robert P. Colwell et al., "Instruction Sets and Beyond: Computers, Complexity, and Controversy," *Computer* (September 1985)

[3] C. V. Ramamoorthy and H. F. Li, "Pipeline Architecture," Tutorial: Computer Architecture (I. E. E. E. Computer Society)

Chapter 3

Reduced-Instruction-Set, Writable-Instruction-Set, and Very-Long-Instruction-Word Computers

REDUCED-INSTRUCTION-SET COMPUTER (RISC)

Philosophy

Instruction sets and their addressing modes and functional classes may grow to be quite complicated. For example, the widely used minicomputer VAX 11/780 has 16 addressing modes and more than 300 unique instructions! Even microprocessors often have complicated instruction sets. The Motorola 68020 recognizes seven data types, employs 18 addressing modes, and uses instruction formats that may vary in length from 1 16-bit word up to 11 16-bit words.

The use of a complicated instruction set requires that the CPU have a complicated instruction decoder and control unit. In the Motorola 68000 family of microprocessors, the control unit occupies more than 60% of the total chip area. This allocation represents a significant portion of the silicon resources in the CPU, and almost all of this expense is incurred to support just the complex instruction set of the processor.

A relatively recent development in CPU architecture design is a philosophy that carefully adapts the instruction set to the capabilities of the silicon data path in the CPU. Instead of going to great lengths to implement complex machine language instructions and addressing modes in silicon, which might simplify assembly language programming and compiler design, this new design philosophy chooses to implement only those instructions that are necessary to create a good, orthogonal, "basic set." Implementation of these few "essential" instructions is carried out in a manner that facilitates or even optimizes the integrated circuit layout, particularly that of the control unit. The optimization always is for maximum speed of execution — typically one system clock cycle for each instruction executed. The philosophy is called reduced-instruction-set computer or RISC architecture.

In contrast to a complex-instruction-set computer (CISC), RISC architectures use carefully chosen, simple-to-lay-out instruction sets to create CPUs and result in systems that have a higher processing throughput and lower ratio of cost to performance.

Evolution

The RISC concepts are not particularly new; their hardware implementation, however, had to await the development of very-large-scale integration (VLSI). Reduced-instruction-set architectures have evolved along the following basic lines.

The early IBM 801 architecture (named for the number of the building in which the team of design engineers worked) was a RISC architecture designed in 1976, although the term *RISC* was not used to identify the system. The IBM Research Office Products Division Microprocessor (ROMP), the IBM PC RT (RISC technology) system, and the Hewlett-Packard Spectrum family of computer systems are to some degree descendants of the IBM 801.

By making CPU processing throughput a driving force at each stage of the design, Seymour Cray created some of the most sophisticated RISC architectures in his CRAY systems [1]. In particular, Cray stressed the use of CPU register operations, pipelined instruction execution, and access of memory only through LOAD/STORE instructions. A descendant of the CRAY technology is the Integraph CLIPPER 32-bit processor.

Development of the RISC I and RISC II devices at the University of California at Berkeley led eventually to the Pyramid 90X system, the Ridge 32, and the Sun SPARC workstation architectures.

At Stanford University, John Hennessy coordinated a team of researchers in the development of the MIPS (microprocessor without interlocked pipeline stages) [2]. This device is a pipelined, 32-bit RISC with two kilobytes of on-chip instruction cache [3]. This research led to the establishment of a private company, MIPS Computer Systems, Inc., whose main products are RISC CPUs, floating-point coprocessors, and workstations. As was the case with Seymour Cray, John Hennessy recognized the vital need for very "smart" optimizing compilers that would force maximum performance from each RISC architecture [4].

In this chapter, we shall examine several of these RISC devices, to identify points that classify them as RISC and to point out unique features.

To avoid confusion when RISC is used as a generic term, the devices developed at Berkeley are identified, in this text, as the Berkeley RISC or as RISC I or II.

Characteristics

General. The definition of RISC architecture is abused often. The number of instructions alone is not an adequate factor to judge the type of architecture that a processor has. As Colwell et al. [5] state: "An example of how the issue of scope can be confused is found in a recent article [6]. By creating a machine with only one instruction, its authors claim to have delimited the RISC design space to their machine at one end of the space and the RISC I (with 31 instructions) at the other end. This model is far too simplistic to be useful; an absolute number of instructions cannot be the sole criterion for categorizing an architecture as to RISC or CISC. It ignores aspects of addressing modes and their associated complexity, fails to deal with compiler/architecture coupling, and provides no way to evaluate the implementation of other non-instruction set design decisions such as register files, caches, memory management, floating-point operations, and co-processors."

The following eight criteria are the basic attributes of RISC architectures.

First, RISC architecture has a relatively low number of primitive or basic instructions, preferably fewer than 100. For example, the RISC I has 31 instructions; the RISC II has 39 instructions; the Stanford MIPS has 31 instructions. Currently available RISC devices, such as the ACORN ARM and the Motorola 88100, reflect this attribute. All other instructions are "synthesized" by the primitive instructions. Furthermore, other operations are register-to-register. This restriction greatly simplifies the RISC hardware design.

Second, there is a relatively low number of addressing modes, usually one or two. Indexed addressing, with an index (offset or displacement) of zero, may be used in place of direct addressing so that, if this type of architecture is designed to use indexed addressing, there is no need also for direct addressing. The absence of complex addressing modes facilitates restarting of instructions that a trap or fault interrupts.

Third, there is a relatively low number of instruction formats, usually one or two. Instructions are of fixed length.

Fourth, all accesses to memory are performed by Load/Store and branch instructions and stack manipulations.

Fifth, to the extent practicable, each instruction executes in one cycle of the system clock. That is, the measure of "clocks per instruction" (CPI) is very nearly unity. This characteristic means that, at the conventional machine level, each instruction is equivalent to a single microoperation.

Sixth, there is a relatively large register file in the CPU. Typically the number is greater than 32. Wherever possible, register-to-register instead of memory-to-register operations are used.

Seventh, the control unit is hardwired, offering simplicity and speed.

Eighth, during the design of the instruction set and architecture, careful attention is paid to the efficient execution of one particular high-level language. For example, the Berkeley RISC processors are "language-directed" toward the C language. The most common high-level language features that affect RISC architectures are:

1. procedure and subroutine linking;

2. local ("automatic") variables; and
3. data types and structures.

The instruction execution pipeline [7] and the organization of the CPU register file are coupled tightly to the design of an optimizing compiler for the "target" high-level language. The goal of this action is to close the so-called semantic gap between high-level and low-level languages. The idea is to minimize the difference between the basic operations provided by the high-level language and those provided by the architecture.

Implementation in the Berkeley RISC

Figures 3–1 and 3–2 depict, respectively, the Berkeley RISC I and RISC II.

The RISC I and II are 32-bit processors since each memory access loads or stores four 8-bit bytes at a time. The memory is byte-addressable, half-word (16-bits) addressable (if the least significant bit of the address is zero), and word-addressable (if the two least significant bits of the address are zero).

The RISC II has a total of 138, on-chip, working registers, R_0 through R_{137}. Register R_0 is permanently wired so that it always contains zero. Consequently, indexed addressing, with R_0 as the index register, serves the same purpose as direct addressing, so that the RISC I and II do not need direct addressing.

Each active process executing on the Berkeley RISC can "see" only 32 of the 138 registers. The process can "see" these 32 registers through a register window dedicated to that purpose. If a process invokes another process, such as a subroutine, a new register window is opened for the new process. Each new register window overlaps the preceding one, as shown in Fig. 3–3. To further optimize this architecture's performance, an overlapping window arrangement is employed. Thus, successive windows have a certain number of registers in common. The registers in the overlapping part of a window are used to pass parameters and arguments between the calling and called procedures. The other registers are used for storage of

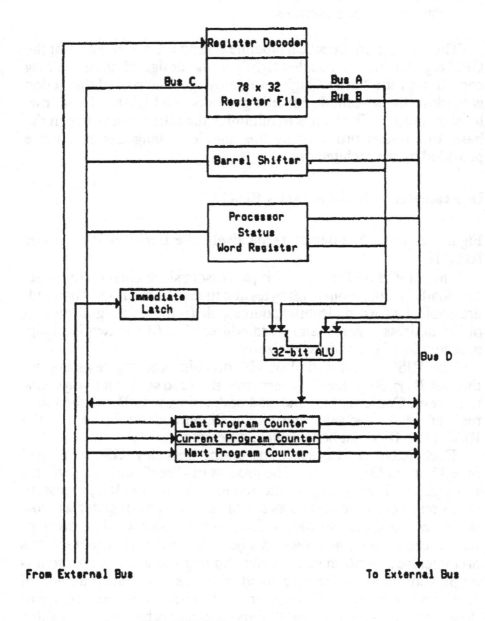

Fig. 3-1. Organization of RISC I

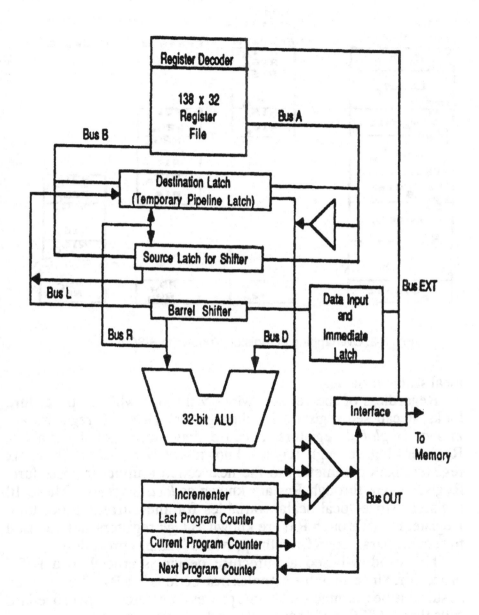

Fig. 3-2. Organization of RISC II

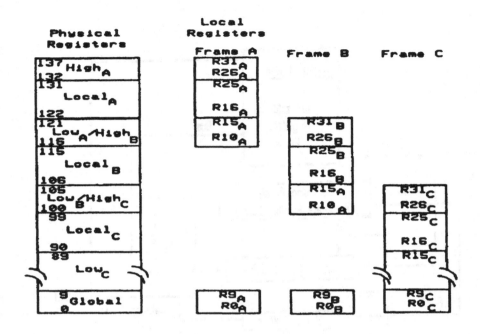

Fig. 3-3. Overlapping of register windows in RISC II

local scalar variables.

Regardless of the register window through which a procedure looks, it can see registers R_0 through R_9. These 10 registers are known as *global* registers, because they store global variables. Registers R_{10} through R_{15} are known as *low* registers. These six registers pass parameters to the next called routine or procedure. Registers R_{16} through R_{25} are known as *local* registers. These 10 registers store local scalar variables for the current procedure. Registers R_{26} through R_{31} are known as *high* registers and are used to receive parameters from the previous (calling) procedure.

The window-based architecture design is crucial to a RISC processor. Since all of the complex instructions in a RISC are treated as subroutines, or macros, a RISC processor creates more procedure calls than a CISC, and those calls are time consuming.

Naturally, a RISC processor may face a problem during nesting of procedures. If the nesting level is deep enough, the RISC processor may handle the overflow condition by creating an additional stack in system memory. Thus, overflow and underflow conditions are handled by associated circuitry in the RISC and with a trap to a software routine that adjusts the procedure stack in memory.

The Berkeley RISCs handle unsigned and signed (2s complement) integers of 8, 16, and 32 bits. A major deficiency of these early RISC devices is their lack of floating-point arithmetic capabilities. However, the purpose of these two devices was to prove a principle and not to develop a commercially marketable product. Currently available devices, such as the Transputer, have floating-point capability.

The Berkeley RISCs do not execute every instruction in exactly one cycle of the clock, but they come close to doing so. In one cycle, these RISCs can add the contents of two registers and store the sum into a third register. This capability is an example of fast, register-to-register arithmetic. All load and store instructions are executed by the Berkeley RISC in one cycle.

The register-to-register instructions and the memory-reference instructions use one format. A 1-bit flag, called SCC, displays the status of the condition codes (set or cleared). A 5-bit destination field identifies either the destination register, R_d, (within the current register window if DEST > 9) or the R_m for STORE instructions. A 5-bit "Source 1" field identifies the first source operand, which is always a register (R_s) for register-to-register operations and an index register (R_x) for memory-access operations.

If the immediate mode flag is not set, the low-order 5 bits of "Source 2" specify the second source register, S_2, if the instruction is register-to-register, or else "Source 2" specifies an offset (or base address) for memory-reference instructions. If the immediate mode flag is set, then "Source 2" is interpreted as the 13 least significant bits of a sign-extended, 2s complement, immediate operand.

Indirect addressing is implemented in two steps, and, as previously noted, direct addressing is implemented as a special case of indexed addressing, in which the index register is R_0.

Figure 3-4 sets out another instruction format, used primarily by the branch instructions. The least significant 19 bits are interpreted as an address relative to the program counter. This address is designated as Y in most of the Berkeley RISC documentation. This format permits the RISC to employ self-relative addressing in procedures that have to be relocated frequently.

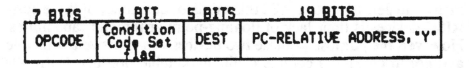

7 BITS	1 BIT	5 BITS	19 BITS
OPCODE	Condition Code Set flag	DEST	PC-RELATIVE ADDRESS, "Y"

Fig. 3-4. Branch instruction format

The Berkeley designers attempted to gain chip area by simplifying the instruction set and thereby reducing the size of the control unit. The gained space is used to implement the register file and the control logic for the overlapping register windows. Certain CISC advocates have argued that it is the overlapping register windows, rather than the reduced instruction set, that give the Berkeley RISC their surprising performance advantages. There would have been, however, insufficient chip space to implement the register windows had it not been for the reduced size of the control unit. That is, RISC is not just a trick that happens to work. It is a radically new architectural design philosophy that must be applied consistently across the entire system.

A number of benchmark programs, written in C and Pascal, have been used to determine the number of global registers, local variables, and passed parameters [8]. The Berkeley RISC design might have turned out differently if its architects had directed it toward another high-level language.

With the Berkeley architecture, a programmer is limited to 9 global variables, 10 local variables, and 6 passed parameters. In descriptions of the Berkeley RISCs, their architects do not elaborate adequately on what steps a programmer should take if more than six parameters need to be passed in a called routine. The large increase in efficiency gained by the presence of the register windows appears to go out the window if there is a frequent need for passing more than six scalar variables between subroutines.

Another important question that arises from the register window concept is how does a subroutine access up-level local variables? An up-level local variable is a scalar variable originally local for a parent, or ancestor, routine but having become global for all descendants of the routine that created that variable. This up-level access is not easy. A compiler must create and maintain an activation table for all subroutines that have not yet RETURNed. The current window pointer (CWP) (actually, 16 x CWP) must have a location in this table. Any memory access to up-level local variables must be translated using the activation table.

If the variable discussed in the previous paragraph is still in the register file, that variable may be found by indexing its register number by 16 x CWP, that is, CWP shifted left 4 bits. If, however, the variable has been stored in memory because of a stack overflow, then the stack overflow handler must modify the current window pointers in the activation table or build a translation lookup table, so that the effective physical memory address may be found. Neither requirement is trivial or efficient. Naturally, if a routine's local variables are never global to its descendants, this situation does not present a problem. That condition, however, is not true for all high-level languages.

Pipelining Caveats

Pipelining concepts are described in Chapter 2. It should be noted, however, that in RISC architectures pipelining must be treated judiciously. A compiler or assembly language programmer for a RISC architecture must be very wise indeed, if the pipeline latencies are not to spoil the average cycles per instruction (CPI). The costs of the pipeline latencies may be reduced if the CPU architect is very careful in selecting the pipeline structures and the methods by which branch conditions are determined.

As always, an architect's goals are to:

1. minimize the number of clock cycles per instruction; and
2. minimize the pipeline latencies.

A compiler designer must provide "smart" pipeline scheduling for the object code, so that the delays due to pipeline latency are minimized. RISC architectures absolutely require that their high-level language compilers know how to schedule the pipeline properly.

The principles of an optimizing compiler also were discussed in Chapter 2. How does an optimizing compiler minimize the pipeline load latency? Normally, such a compiler seeks to find a nearby instruction that is independent of the original load instruction. Then the compiler places that instruction into a delay slot — i.e., the instruction is relocated (the instruction sequence is reorganized) so that it becomes the instruction immediately after a load instruction. The following example should help to clarify this principle.

Suppose that the following source code executes two independent sums:

$$C := A + B \quad \text{and} \quad F := D + E$$

A compiler generates the following sequence of instructions:

```
LOAD R1,A
LOAD R2,B
ADD R3,R1,R2
LOAD R4,D
LOAD R5,E
ADD R6,R4,R5
```

where Rn is the number of a register. The ADD instructions in this example will "stall" — i.e., they will generate a pipeline timing hazard that will cause the pipeline interlock, if any, to introduce wait states into the execution flow. This action results because all of the needed operands have not yet been computed.

If the pipeline load latency is one cycle and the optimizing compiler is sufficiently "smart," then one of the LOAD instructions that is independent from the ADD operation may be inserted into the delay slot as follows:

```
LOAD R1,A
LOAD R2,B
LOAD R4,D
ADD R3,R1,R2
LOAD R5,E
ADD R6,R4,R5
```

The result is the elimination of the pipeline wait states. Such an optimizing compiler is, therefore, intelligent enough to take full advantage of the RISC architecture and its pipeline, whenever it is possible to do so.

If it is impossible to locate an independent instruction to insert into the delay slot, then a no-operation (NOP) instruction must be used, naturally at the expense of execution efficiency.

An optimizing compiler may counteract pipeline branch latency by one of two methods: delayed branches or canceling branches.

In the case of a delayed branch, those instructions (one or more) that immediately follow the branch instruction are always executed, whether or not the branch is performed. These instructions occupy the "branch latency" slots. For example, if the branch latency is two cycles, then the two one-cycle instructions (or perhaps, one two-cycle instruction) immediately after the branch are executed always.

Consider the following portion of a program:

```
LOAD R1,A
LOAD R2,B
ADD R5,R3,R4
BEQ R5,0,LABEL
        ...
LABEL: {execution continues here if R5 = 0}.
```

Notice that the first two LOAD instructions are independent of the branch test and that they both are executed whether or not the branch is performed. A good RISC optimizing compiler detects this fact and reorganizes the sequence as follows:

    ADD R5,R3,R4
    BEQ R5,0,LABEL
    LOAD R1,A
    LOAD R2,B

       ...
LABEL: {execution continues here if R5 = 0}

Now the two LOAD instructions still are executed, but they have been moved into the branch latency slots so that there is no pipeline stalling (wait states or NOPs) resulting from the branch. Again, an optimizing compiler must know when and where to employ this scheme.

In the case of a canceling branch design, the instructions in the delay slots are canceled if the branch is performed. Canceling branches sometimes are called *nullifying* or *squashing* branches because of the way in which they must undo the effects of those instructions present in the latency slots (if the branch is performed).

Another form of a canceling branch undoes the instructions after the branch instruction only if the branch is not performed. Basically, an optimizing compiler predicts whether a branch will be performed. This action works fairly well because, in software, most branches are performed much more frequently than not. For example, many branches close loops in the code, and so the branch back to the top of the loop is performed on all but one pass (the last) through the loop.

It should be clear that the task of branch delay minimization is difficult. Advocates of RISC architectures are confident that, eventually, "smart" optimizing compilers will be designed so that the full potential of RISC processors may be realized in real-world applications. An optimizing compiler must have the capability to "pool-up" a list of "safe" and, in the case of delayed branches, useful instructions that may be moved into the branch latency slots. The design of such a compiler is not easy, but the resulting increase in processor performance can be dramatic.

Notice that the use of canceling branches increases the number of "safe" instructions in the pool; however, the cancellation itself introduces a certain amount of undesired overhead.

Most RISC architectures rely primarily on the "intelligence" of an optimizing compiler taking advantage of the potential power of the architectures [9]. A typical optimizing compiler normally compiles the high-level language source code as an assembly-level pseudocode (P code). After that task, actual optimization commences. The pseudocode is merged with library procedures and modules (if any are required) and with other execution-time tools or toolset calls. Then a series of local optimizations and pipeline scheduling operations are performed. Full global optimization is performed next.

At this point, approximately 50% or more of a compiler's time is consumed with complex intraprocedural and interprocedural register allocations, so that, whenever possible, the pipeline latency slots may be filled with useful instructions. Finally, all of the compiled procedures are merged by a linker into a self-contained object module.

In addition to optimizing pipeline latencies, six other specific optimization methods that a compiler uses may be described: register allocation, redundancy elimination, loop optimization, speedup, branch-to-branch elimination, and strength reduction [10].

In register allocation, a compiler attempts to maintain frequently used data in the register file, thereby reducing the number of load/store operations.

With redundancy elimination, a compiler attempts to find opportunities to reuse rather than recompute results. This method eliminates redundant computations.

In loop optimization, variable values and expressions that do not change during a loop are moved outside the loop so that they do not have to be reevaluated each time a pass is made through the loop.

During speedup, a compiler searches for any, usually local, situation in which a slow operation may be sped up through use of an alternative method of computation. For example, to multiply a value by the constant $14_{10} = 1110_2$, a compiler may substitute for the normal and, consequently, lengthy operation of multiplication, the following steps:

1. shift left 3 bits (equivalent to multiplying by 8);
2. subtract the multiplicand from the result of the shift (equivalent to multiplying by 7); and
3. shift the result of the subtraction left 1 bit (equivalent to multiplying by 14).

In the branch-to-branch elimination method, if the target of a branch instruction is another branch instruction, the target address of the first branch instruction may be changed to that of the second branch instruction.

The strength-reduction method reflects that, sometimes, a time-consuming operation may be replaced by a less time-consuming one. For example, the index into a multidimensional array frequently is computed with several multiplications and additions. Strength reduction will attempt to reduce the complexity of this index calculation by using a previously calculated address and a simple addition.

The design of the instruction set itself also may be useful in minimizing branch delays. For example, a branch condition need not be generated by a branch instruction. Before a branch, other instructions may set up condition codes or flags. Typically these are arithmetic or logical compares.

Motorola 88100

A cursory inspection of the 88100 reveals that, in its internal organization, several features that tend to slow down the operation of a conventional microprocessor either have been replaced by dedicated circuits (for example, multipliers) or have been increased in number, to reduce loss of speed.

Striking facts observed in the internal organization of the MC88100 are multiplicity of pipelining and a high degree of parallelism. One may think that, with such added features, the organization of the 88100 is complicated. The illustration in Fig. 3–5 exemplifies that, instead, the organization appears rather "clean." Various independent units are used in the fetching and execution, each of which contains its own complex but independent logic. We shall return to these independent units later.

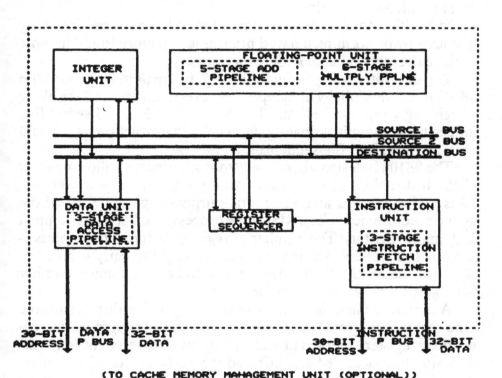

Fig. 3-5. Internal organization of the Motorola 88100

Pipelining is used extensively in the 88100. We have discussed, however, how costly an inadequately designed pipeline scheme can be. We also have discussed that there is a certain amount of latency in pipelining. Most processors employ only one pipeline, for example, for instruction-address calculation, fetching, and decoding. The penalties for change-of-flow instructions are obvious in this case.

Some form of invalidation or clearing of the pipeline needs to be performed, causing a processor delay. After the pipeline is cleared or "flushed," additional time is required for startup of the pipeline. In the 88100, the presence of four pipelines significantly reduces this problem. The floating-point unit has a five-stage add pipeline and a six-stage multiply pipeline.

In addition to abundant pipelines, the 88100 reduces pipelining latencies by performing delayed branching, a feature found in most of the currently available RISC processors.

The next interesting feature that adds to the performance of the 88100 is the multiplicity of independent execution units, which allow a high degree of parallelism. The schematic in Fig. 3–5 shows five units: an integer unit; a floating-point unit; an instruction unit; a data unit; and a register file/sequencer.

The 88100 is designed as a load/store architecture, allowing most of the instructions to be executed within registers. The 88100 contains 51 instructions and 32 general-purpose registers. One of the generic requirements for a RISC-type processor is that it be equipped with many registers. The number of registers within a microprocessor obviously affects its performance. During the early simulation stages of the 88100, 32 registers proved to be an optimum number for high-performance applications.

A number of facts led the Motorola designers to this conclusion. One fact was the analysis of high-level language programs that execute on register-oriented processors. It was discovered that an overflow situation occurred and affected the performance of compilers during the control of data allocation on a large number of registers, such as 128. It was physically impossible to maintain track of the number. When the number of registers exceeds, e.g., 25, compiler performance begins to decrease as the number of registers increases.

One also must think of the structural and electrical limitations, such as drive capability and fan-out of the decoder, affected by capacitive loading. These are affected adversely as the number of registers increases. The results are slower access time of registers and slower clock frequency.

An additional adverse effect of an overabundance of registers is that the number of bits in the opcode word required to decode a register becomes greater and, thus, places a restriction on the size of immediate data values.

A feature that adds to the overall performance of the 88100 is the presence of three parallel buses, two for the source operands and one for the destination of the result. The three buses transfer data to the execution units and the registers, all of which are 32 bits wide. The bus activity is monitored and controlled by the sequencer unit.

The floating-point unit carries out all the internal floating-point operations. The 88100 is capable of executing up to five floating-point instructions and six floating-point or integer-multiply instructions at the same time as up to three data memory accesses and three instruction fetches. Thus, in addition to the execution of all floating-point instructions, the FPU manipulates integer/floating-point conversions and integer multiplication and division instructions. One may ask why, if an integer unit already exists within the processor, does the FPU handle also integer operations? The answer is that this action allows the integer unit to carry out many instructions in a single clock cycle, leaving the multiple-cycle instructions to be executed by the more complex arithmetic-logic unit in the FPU.

The floating-point unit then executes a number of instructions that do not complete in one cycle, such as single-precision addition, subtraction, and conversion instructions, which consume five cycles, and multiplication instructions, which require six. Division instructions are the only floating-point operations that are not completely pipelined. A division instruction executes by looping through one stage of the pipeline for each bit of required accuracy.

The 88100 can execute a number of floating-point instructions on each consecutive clock cycle by proper scheduling of floating-point and integer addition and division instructions.

The remaining integer arithmetic and bit field instructions, logical instructions, and control register instructions are executed by the integer unit. This unit also has charge of all of the operations required for memory-addressing calculations and program sequencing.

Although not shown in Fig. 3-5, the internal structure of the integer unit consists of three separate functional subunits that contribute to increased throughput. A bit-field unit executes all bit-field instructions. All integer arithmetic instructions and logical instructions are executed by a 32-bit arithmetic-logic unit. Finally, a separate branch unit calculates branch offsets, allowing the implementation of delayed branching for all branch instructions. This separation of tasks within the integer unit provides a significant degree of parallelism, because three of these operations can be executed concurrently in different registers. A compiler designed to monitor register activity very carefully can take considerable advantage of this type of concurrency.

The register file/sequencer serves several tasks. The file contains the 32 general-purpose registers. The only restrictions on use of these registers are for register R_0 and R_1. When accessed, R_0 returns zero. This feature is advantageous, particularly to clear register contents quickly during program initialization, because R_0 can be transferred to any other registers within the register file. The restriction imposed upon R_1 is that it be used to hold the return address of a branch to a subroutine.

To allow concurrent access to the register file, three ports exist. Two receive their input from the two source buses, and the third port acts as an output to the destination bus. To increase instruction throughput, the 88100 employs a feed-forward information technique, very useful for multiple register use. This technique transfers the destination result from the current operation required for execution by the next instruction on one of the source buses and, thus, ensures that the unit waiting for data receives them as soon as possible. The same technique is applied if both source registers are in use and may be modified by the previous instruction; both operands can be received by feed-forward. The way by which the technique is implemented enables prioritizing of register writes from the execution units. One-cycle instructions are assigned the highest priority, with the floating-point unit and the data unit following.

The sequencer satisfies one of the requirements of RISC architecture; that is, this circuit is hardwired rather than microprogrammed. The sequencer controls register access, arbitration of the internal buses, and exception arbitration. Furthermore, the sequencer generates all of the control signals for the instruction unit and internal buses.

A significant task of the sequencer is tracking the particular register in use at any given time. Due to the parallel execution nature of the 88100, more than one execution unit can gain independent access to the register file. To reduce potential confusion of the system, the 88100 is equipped with a scoreboard register. This register maintains a bit for each general-purpose register that is in use, other than R_0, which, as noted, constantly contains a zero and cannot be modified. All instructions that consume more than one cycle cause the scoreboard bit or bits that correspond to the destination register or registers to be set. This technique inhibits, during parallel instruction execution, destruction of the contents of source registers that have not yet been computed from a previous instruction. Due to this technique, the 88100 is not restricted to complete execution of one instruction before commencement of execution of another.

The role of the sequencer in exception handling is significant. The 88100 generates two types of exceptions: precise and imprecise. The exact processor context at the time a precise exception occurs is available, as is the exact cause of the exception. For example, interrupts and bus errors are precise exceptions that include all of the information required for the complete recovery of the 88100 from the exception. On the other hand, when an imprecise exception is processed, the exact processor context is unknown because concurrent operations have affected the information that makes up the processor context. Thus, an overflow of the floating-point unit causes an imprecise exception, in which case the entire context is not needed for recovery from the exception, if the operation in progress is known.

It is thus obvious that the function of the sequencer in exception handling can affect the performance of the 88100. The sequencer must be able to act on all pending precise exceptions before handling imprecise ones. The latter require investigation by the exception servicing routine.

Before transfer to the appropriate execution unit, instructions are fetched from the instruction bus by the instruction unit, which also carries out the first stages of instruction decoding.

The instruction unit is designed with a three-stage pipeline and three instruction pointers that indicate the contents of the execution pipeline. The first of the pointers, the execution instruction pointer (xip), points to the instruction in current execution in the integer unit, data unit, or floating-point unit. The second pointer, the next instruction pointer (nip), points to the instruction currently being accessed from memory or the memory-management unit and decoded for execution. The third pointer, the fetch instruction pointer (fip), points to the memory location of the next instruction to be fetched.

Due to the external bus operation, data are fetched on the clock following the address. Therefore, during this phase, the fip contains the address of the next instruction. The three-stage pipeline scheme is advantageous for prefetching instructions before the 88100 is ready to use those instructions. The scheme also facilitates recovery from an erroneous bus access.

The data unit is equipped with a 30-bit dedicated calculation unit for addresses and a three-stage pipeline. The main functions of the data unit are execution of instructions that access data memory and control of the data-interface portion of the data P bus.

The required address for fetching is calculated in stage 2 of the pipeline. Stage 1 drives the external data-address bus. If the access is a store operation, stage 1 fetches data from registers and drives the external data bus. Stage 0 of the pipeline monitors the response of external memory. For a store operation, the data bus is read and, for a write operation, a register in the register file is loaded.

The register complement of the 88100 is shown in Fig. 3–6. After the reset procedure, the 88100 enters the supervisor mode, in which all registers are available for programming, and the hardware resources of the 88100 can be configured for a desired application. In user mode, the control registers are protected against erroneous accessing, thus avoiding system corruption. In user mode, the general-purpose registers are used to program the 88100.

Generally, the supervisor mode is limited to kernel-type software, and thus only a small amount of very fast exception-handling code is accessed in this mode. While in the supervisor mode, the 88100 can be programmed to perform a number of functions. For

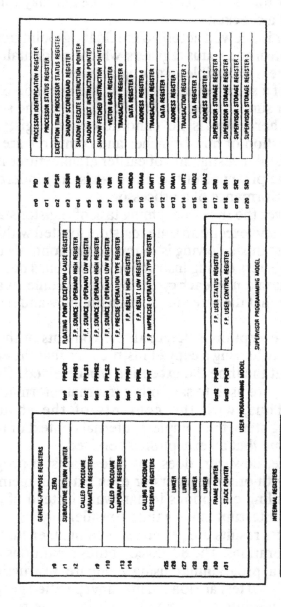

Fig. 3-6. 88100 programming model

example, for fault-tolerant applications, the 88100 may function as either a master or a checker.

A programmer is allowed access to the floating-point unit via the floating-point control and status registers, which, incidentally, are the only control registers accessible to a programmer.

The absence of a stack pointer brings up the question of how interrupts and other similar tasks are handled in either the supervisor or user mode. There also is no condition-code register, which generates the question of how branches and compares are handled by the 88100. Careful investigation of earlier architectures led to the conclusion that the presence of these two registers hindered rather than aided the performance of a processor.

The 88100 solves the time-consuming task of register stacking by the use of shadow and exception time registers located within the integer unit. The aim of shadowing is to record the contents of the internal pipeline registers during instruction execution. That is, a copy of these registers is taken on each cycle; the copied contents are simply the information that the three instruction pointers and scoreboard register hold.

Whenever an exception is detected, the contents of the shadow registers are frozen, leaving a copy of instructions that the 88100 was about to execute at the time the exception was detected. The exception-time registers are used to save other internal information at exception time. Thus, with the contents of the shadow and exception-time registers, the complete internal context of the 88100 is known at the time that an exception is serviced.

This technique, however, does not rule against a programmer creating a stack with other registers or even external memory. The technique of handling exceptions in hardware instead of a regular stack reduces the interrupt latency time considerably.

Conditional test results are generated in a manner that complements parallel operations. The 88100 computes conditions at the explicit request of a programmer using compare instructions. The results of a conditional test are loaded into any specified general-purpose register and not into a dedicated condition-code register, thus eliminating contention between concurrent execution units accessing a dedicated condition-code register. If, e.g., the 88100 had a dedicated condition-code register, evaluation of the result of a compare instruction would imply that one instruction has higher priority than another in terms of accessing the results of the condition-code register. If this were indeed the case, then the second instruction would be required to suspend execution until the higher priority instruction had no further use of the condition-code register. More often than not, the presence of a dedicated condition-code register in a processor whose internal organization is structured toward concurrent processing is undesirable.

Rather than a dedicated condition-code register, the 88100 employs a string of predicates that can be evaluated in any of the general-purpose registers. So long as the destination register in which a predicate is being evaluated is not used by instructions that follow, then a string of compare or branchlike instructions can execute without delay. The complete set of the predicates used are shown in Fig. 3-7.

Higher than or same	Greater than or equal	Not equal
Lower than	Less than	Equal
Lower than or same	Less than or equal	Uncomparable
Higher than	Greater than	Comparable

Fig. 3-7. Predicates used in condition testing

The 88100 manipulates three types of instructions: flow-control, data memory access, and register-to-register. The first type changes the sequential flow of instructions through the 88100. This class of instructions corresponds to so-called program control instructions in other processors, such as jump and branch. The second type handles the transfer of data between memory and general-purpose registers.

The third type corresponds to data-handling instructions in other processors; that is, register-to-register instructions manipulate data held by the general-purpose registers. All instructions are 32 bits in length.

The 88100 uses a triadic addressing mode system. Three 5-bit fields in the instruction specify two source registers each and a destination register. However, all three of the specified registers need not be used.

The register-to-register modes in the 88100 include the register mode with 10-bit immediate addressing, which manipulates bit-field instructions. These instructions allow the 88100 to operate on individual bits of information. The format of this mode is shown in Fig. 3-8.

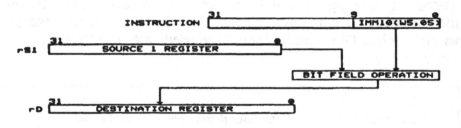

Fig. 3-8. Register-to-register mode

In this case, the 10-bit literal field in the bottom bits of the instruction opcode (IMM10) contains the width and the offset of the bit field on which the source register, $S1$, is to act.

The other register-to-register mode is the register mode with 16-bit immediate addressing. In this addressing mode, the contents of source register $S1$ are added to a 16-bit literal value of the opcode to produce the destination result, as shown in Fig. 3–9. This form of addressing is used by arithmetic and logical instructions that require an immediate value.

The 88100 has three data memory access modes.

In the mode register indirect with zero-extended immediate, shown in Fig. 3–10, the contents of source register $S1$ are added to the 16-bit offset held in the lower 16 bits of the instruction opcode.

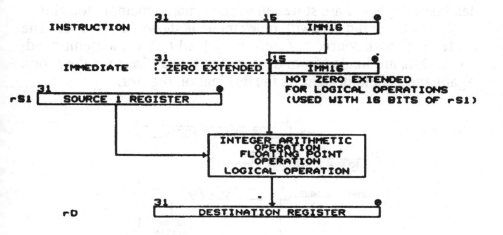

Fig. 3-9. Register mode with 16-bit immediate addressing

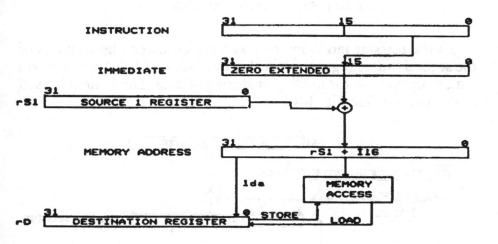

Fig. 3-10. Register indirect with zero-extended immediate

The sum is a data memory address to which data are stored or from which data are loaded, in both cases via the P bus. For a load instruction, data are loaded into the register specified by the D(estination) field of the instruction. For a store instruction, data contained in the destination register are stored in the designated memory location.

The register indirect with index mode is shown in Fig. 3–11. The contents of both source registers are added to form a memory address. Data are loaded from or stored to that address via the P bus. Again, the D field designates the destination register.

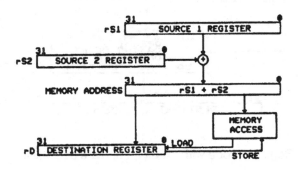

Fig. 3-11. Register indirect with index

In the register mode indirect with scaled index, the contents of the second source register are scaled by a factor of 1, 2, 4, or 8 to form a memory address for loading or storing of data. The D field is used as destination. See Fig. 3–12.

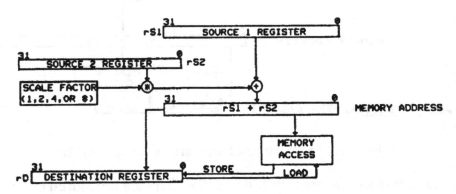

Fig. 3-12. Register indirect with scaled index

The three flow-control modes of the 88100 are the register with 9-bit vector table index, the register with 16-bit displacement/immediate, and the 26-branch displacement.

The register mode with 9-bit vector table index, shown in Fig. 3–13, is used, during processing of an exception, to place a value in the fetch-instruction pointer corresponding to the exception-vector address. The mode concatenates the 9-bit vector offset for the exception with the vector base registers to produce the final fetch-instruction pointer. At reset, the vector base register is programmed to an address corresponding to the memory location in which the exception vectors are placed. For a trap-on-condition exception, 5 bits in the instruction opcode are tested and, only if these bits are true, is a new value loaded into the fetch-instruction pointer.

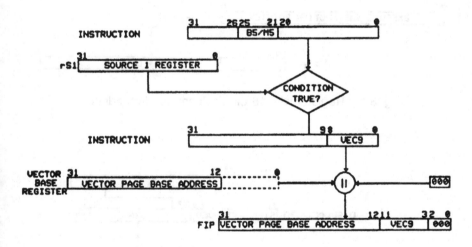

Fig. 3-13. Register with 9-bit vector table index

Branch and trap instructions use the register mode with 16-bit displacement/immediate, for target-address and test-condition generation. In this mode, source register $S1$ is tested. If the branch or trap condition is true, the 16-bit offset is added to the execution instruction pointer and placed in the fetch-instruction pointer. Figure 3–14 depicts this mode.

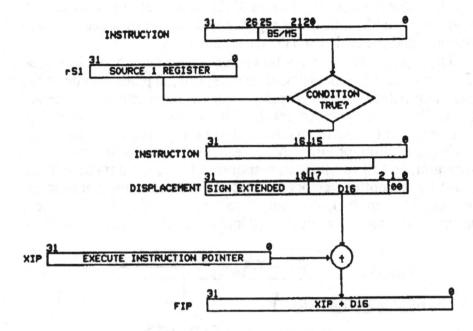

Fig. 3-14. Register with 16-bit displacement/immediate

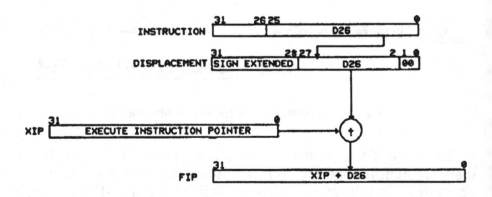

Fig. 3-15. The 26-branch displacement

The 26-branch displacement mode, shown in Fig. 3–15, is used by branch instructions to specify the branch target address. The 26-bit offset in the instruction opcode is added to the execution-instruction pointer to produce the content of the fetch-instruction pointer.

Control register mode is a type of addressing used to access the general control and floating-point unit control registers. General-purpose registers are loaded from, stored to, or exchanged with the control registers using this mode.

Mention has been made of the P bus. Access to both program and data memory is accomplished via two processor buses, the P buses.

Data accesses are carried out via a 30-bit, data-address bus, DA_{2-31}, and a 32-bit, data bus, D_{0-31}. However, since the 88100 accesses data in the form of only aligned words, the P bus for address generation corresponds to an addressing range of 4 gigabytes.

To support accesses in one clock cycle, the P buses have been designed to be fast and, indeed, operate in one clock cycle. Most microprocessors operate by first driving the address bus, qualifying the addresses with a strobe signal (e.g., Address Latch Enable in the 8085 and Address Strobe in the 68000), reading from or writing to memory, and, finally, waiting for an acknowledgment from the memory device before termination of the cycle. Obviously, with this type of bus operation, a processor needs to wait for a period longer than one clock cycle between accesses.

The P bus can assert addresses on each clock and drive or read the data bus on each clock. Latching of the acknowledgment occurs after the cycle, so that the 88100 is not slowed. A delay occurs only in the presence of a fault. All P bus activity is synchronized to the processor clock cycle, so that the requirement to supply strobing qualifying signals is eliminated, thus simplifying the external control logic.

The AMD Processors

Chapter 5 is devoted to Advanced Micro Devices' Am29000 stream-lined processor. The company, however, manufactures two other families of RISC processors: the bipolar Am29300 and the CMOS Am29C300.

In actuality, the processors are the same; the fabrication technology varies. The integrated circuits in these two families are usable for design of 32-bit, fixed-word length, RISC chip sets. The Am29334 four-port, dual-register file, the Am29332 Arithmetic-Logic Unit, and the AM29337 bounds checker form the bases for such a design. The ALU includes a barrel shifter and a 64-bit-in, 32-bit-out, funnel shifter.

The AMD design closely resembles that of the Berkeley RISC I processor. Basic to both of these processors is a fixed-instruction format. All instructions in the AMD design are 32 bits in length, as shown in Fig. 3–16. The opcode occupies a field of 7 bits, while three more fields, totalling 23 more bits, specify two source operands and a destination. These fields always occupy the same bits in the instruction opcode format, so that decoding of the opcode in parallel with the operand access is simple.

OPCODE (7 BITS)	SCC (1 BIT)	DESTINATION (5 BITS)	SOURCE 1 (5 BITS)	IMM (1 BIT)	SOURCE 2 (13 BITS)

SCC • SET CONDITION CODE
IMM • IMMEDIATE

Fig. 3-16. Instruction format of the AMD RISC

The overall design of the AMD RISC approach is shown in Fig. 3–17. Delayed branching is used, and exceptions are handled via three registers in the program counter unit. When an exception occurs, the contents of the pipeline are duplicated in these three registers. The program counter unit is routed to the ALU via the A multiplexer, a feature that allows the return address to be saved when a call instruction is executed. During exception handling, this path also enables the processor to save the contents of the three program counter registers so that the contents may be used during a possible restart of the processor.

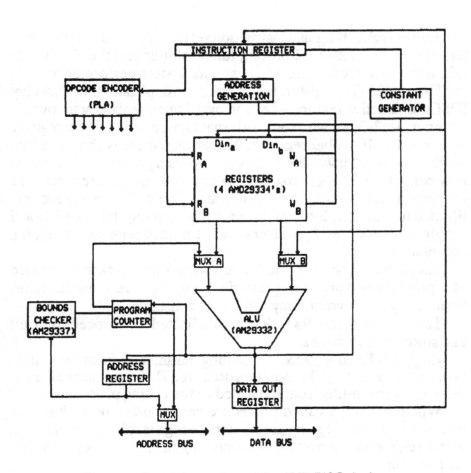

Fig. 3-17. General overview of the AMD RISC design

The instruction set permits direct formation of constants through the instruction word. Before a constant can be transferred to the ALU, however, some data have to be rerouted to create the constant. This rerouting process is carried out by the constant generator, which essentially uses 32 two-input multiplexers. The resultant constant then is transferred to the 32-bit ALU via the B multiplexer.

The processor's control unit is relatively simple. All of the control signals are derived from the instruction's seven-bit opcode via a programmable logic array (PLA).

A powerful, orthogonal instruction set provides a high data-transfer rate. The 64-bit-in, 32-bit-out, funnel shifter and the 32-bit barrel shifter contained in the ALU enhance system performance.

The Am29334 register file is used to duplicate the Berkeley RISCs' distinctive feature — i.e., the overlapped register windows.

Four Am29334s, with some external logic, provide seven register windows and 10 global registers. The arrangement is shown in Fig. 3–18a. One register window is allocated to each procedure. Each window consists of 32 registers; thus, at any time, only 32 registers are visible to a currently executing procedure. These 32 registers are partitioned functionally into four groups: 10 global registers and 10 local registers, as well as 6 registers each for incoming and outgoing parameters.

The global registers R_{22} to R_{31} are shared among each procedure of a program and are used primarily for globally referenced items, such as a system's commonly applicable constants.

The local registers R_6 to R_{15} are dedicated to a procedure itself and store local variables.

Registers R_0 to R_5 accept incoming parameters from the calling procedure for use by the called procedure. These registers also are used to return results from the called to the calling procedure.

When, in turn, a called procedure calls another procedure, the former places its outgoing parameters in registers R_{16} through R_{21}. These registers then overlap the incoming R_0 through R_5 of the latter procedure.

The register arrangement of the AMD RISC permits fast transfer of parameters between procedures, as illustrated in Fig. 3–18b. When procedure A calls procedure B, all of the parameters pass through the outgoing parameter registers of A to become the incoming parameter registers of B. The latter can operate on these parameters without accessing the stack. The same process can go into effect when procedure B calls C. Upon completion of C, the results return via the outgoing parameters of B (or incoming of C). In turn, B also returns its results via the outgoing parameters of A.

To accomplish the window scheme in the AMD RISC, register numbering is the 1s complement of the Berkeley RISC, as shown in

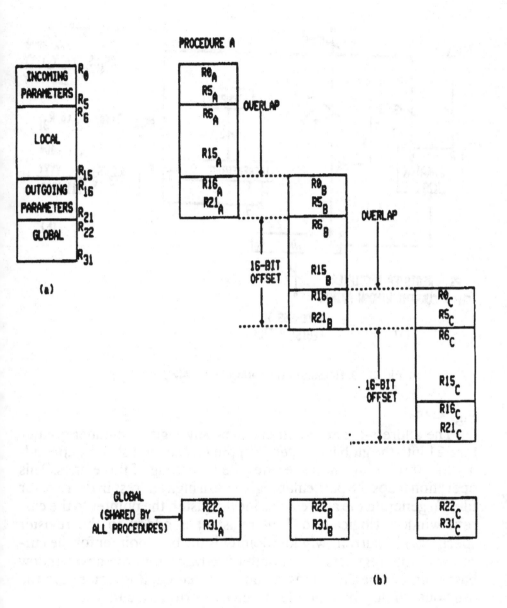

Fig. 3-18. Register window arrangement of the AMD RISC

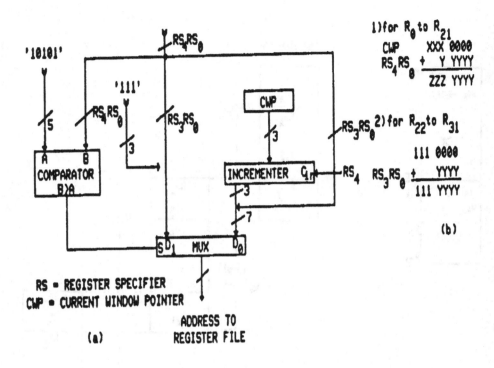

Fig. 3-19. Register numbering in the AMD RISC

Fig. 3–19a.

The address-generation logic maps any register number greater than 21 into the global register. Mapping is accomplished by appending the lower 4 bits of the register file to a string of three ones. This operation maps the particular register to a high address in the register file. To generate the address of a local register, the pointer to the current window (logically a 7-bit register) is added to the register specifier. The current-window pointer is the base pointer for the currently visible registers. The pointer is advanced to the next window base pointer when a call instruction is executed; it is restored to the previous window base pointer when a return is executed.

Since each register window is offset from the previous window by 16 registers, due to the overlap shown in Fig. 3–18b, the lower 4 bits of the current-window pointer are always zero. Therefore, an incrementer at the 5th bit position of this pointer can be used to add in the register specifier. Thus, connection of the 5th bit of the register specifier to the carry-in of the current-window pointer's incrementer generates the proper address for R_0 through R_{21}.

The comparator generates the proper select signals to gate the appropriate address, either local or global, to the register file.

The register file, part of the system's run-time stack, is mapped into the main memory, as shown in Fig. 3–19b. The Am29337 bounds checker detects any memory reference to this section and informs the processor, which then can redirect the reference to the proper data store in the register file.

The MIPS Processor

The acronym MIPS stands for microprocessor without interlocked pipeline stages. This processor is the result of the work of a team at Stanford University under the direction of Prof. John Hennessy, an early advocate of RISC.

At one point, both the Berkeley RISC team and the Stanford team walked on a similar path — symbolic processing. However, while the Berkeley team customized its chip to symbolic-processing languages, such as Smalltalk and LISP, the ultimate goal of the Stanford team was high performance in the execution of compiled code. The Stanford result was the processor shown in Fig. 3–20.

A new version of the MIPS, called MIPS-XMP, has been designed to run at 20 MIPS; produced prototypes run at 17 MIPS (the term MIPS used in both cases here is coincidental; the latter use denotes million instructions per second). Of the 125,000 transistors on the chip, only 25,000 to 30,000 are nonmemory functions. The remainder includes a large on-chip cache and 32 general-purpose registers.

The MIPS employs the following resources:

1. a high-speed, 32-bit, carry look-ahead ALU with hardware support for multiplication and division and a barrel shifter;
2. two 32-bit, bidirectional buses, each connecting almost all of

the functional components;

3. 16 32-bit, general purpose registers;

4. two memory interfaces, one for instruction and one for data (a Harvard-type approach); and

5. an incrementable multistage program counter unit with storage of one branch target address as well as four previous PC values, all of which are required to pipeline instructions and to handle interrupts and exceptions.

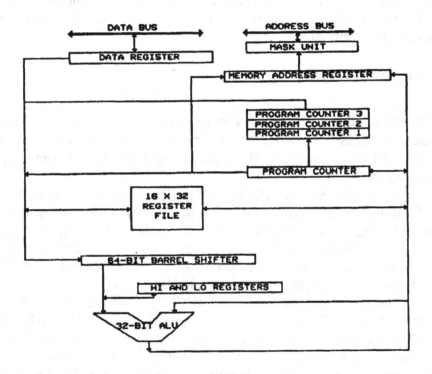

Fig. 3-20. Organization of the Stanford MIPS

All instructions are 32 bits in length. The user instruction set is a so-called compiler-based encoding of the micromachine — i.e., code generation efficiency is used to choose alternative instructions. Multiple, simple, and possibly unrelated instruction "pieces" (groups) are packed together into an instruction word.

The first group consists of ALU pieces, all register-to-register, two and three operand formats. They all use less than half of an instruction word. This group includes byte insert/extract, 2-bit Booth multiplication step, and 1-bit nonrestoring division step.

The second group comprises load/store pieces, which use between 16 and 32 bits of an instruction word. When a load instruction is less than 32 bits, the instruction may be packed with an ALU instruction, which is executed during the execution stage of the pipeline.

The third group, control-flow pieces, includes jumps and compare instructions with relative jumps. The MIPS does not employ condition codes (remember the weaknesses of condition coding in RISC), but includes a rich collection of set conditional and compare and jump instructions.

The fourth group is special pieces. These instructions support procedure and interrupt linkage. The procedure linkage instructions also fit easily into the micromachine format of effective-address calculation and register-to-register computation instructions.

MIPS is a word-addressing machine; the number of instructions, however, is a little on the high side.

Although the MIPS is a pipelined processor, it does not employ hardware pipeline interlocks; hence its name. The five-stage pipeline contains three active instructions at any instant of operation. The MIPS pipeline is divided into an odd-even scheme; either the odd or even pipestages are active.

In a pipelined processor, interlocks are required because of pipeline dependencies. However, hardware need not provide these interlocks. In the MIPS, interlocks are provided by a "pipeline reorganizer." The advantages are twofold. The first is more consistent and faster implementation of hardware, as a result of the absence of complexity usually found in a pipelined processor. Hardware interlocking schemes produce delays, high complexity, and irregularity. The second advantage results because rearrangement of operations at compile-time (we have already discussed how an optimizing compiler functions) is better than their delay until run time. When a processor employs a good reorganizer, most instances in which interlocks are avoidable should be found and utilized. This approach reduces the delay of using available resources.

The design and prototyping of the MIPS-XMP resulted in the establishment of a commmercial venture, MIPS Computer Systems, Inc., in which Professor Hennessy has participated as a chief scientist while maintaining his academic position at Stanford.

Hewlett-Packard SPECTRUM

Hewlett-Packard reportedly has its own RISC processor. In fact, it has called the product a processor "beyond RISC." H-P plans to use this processor as the building block for all of its computers. Due to the secrecy with which H-P usually shields its custom processors, this author has been unable to learn any technical details about the SPECTRUM.

ACORN ARM (VL86C010)

ARM is an acronym for ACORN RISC machine. Its official name is VL86C010.

This device was designed and is produced by the British company ACORN, currently a subsidiary of the Italian typewriter and microcomputer manufacturing giant Olivetti. Interestingly enough, although the ARM is a product of ACORN, it is manufactured by the U.S. company VLSI Technology, Inc., of San Jose, California.

ACORN intended to design a microprocessor that would fit the artificial intelligence specifications of a fifth-generation computer project called ALVEY.

The block diagram of the ARM is shown in Fig. 3–21. Notice the separate Booth's multiplier — multiplication in conventional microprocessors consumes a significant amount of time. ARM has a 32-bit data bus, 27 32-bit registers, the load/store architecture common to most RISC processors, and a partially overlapping register set. The manufacturer claims performance of from five to six million instructions per second.

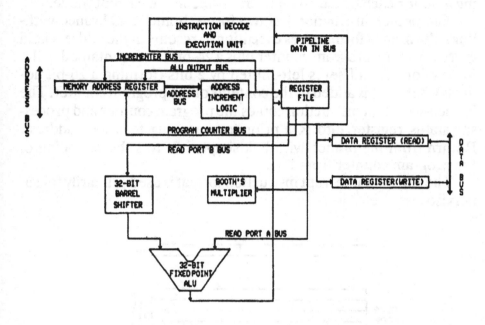

Fig. 3-21.Organization of the ARM

The register file of the ARM is shown in Fig. 3–22. A programmer can access only 16 of the 27 registers. Of the registers, 15 are general-purpose, and 12 are dedicated to such functions as user mode, interrupt request mode, and supervisor mode. The ARM has a combined program counter/processor status register.

The ARM supports five basic types of instructions (all 32 bits long, aligned on word boundaries): data processing, data transfer, block data transfer, branch, and software interrupt. All instructions contain a 4-bit condition execution field that can cause an instruction to be skipped if the condition specified is not true.

The data processing instructions operate only on the register file and use a triadic register addressing mode—i.e., two source and one destination registers.

The block data transfer instructions allow multiple registers to be moved by a single instruction. Such an instruction has a field containing a bit for each of the 16 registers visible in the current mode.

The branch instruction has two forms, branch and branch-with-link. The branch form causes execution to resume at the address held currently in the program counter plus a 24-bit offset contained in the instruction. The offset is left-shifted by 2 bits (forming a 26-bit address), before it is added to the contents of the program counter. The branch-with-link instruction copies the program counter and processor status register into R14 prior to branching to a new address. Return from the branch-with-link simply involves the reloading of the program counter from R14.

The software interrupt instruction format is used primarily for supervisor service calls.

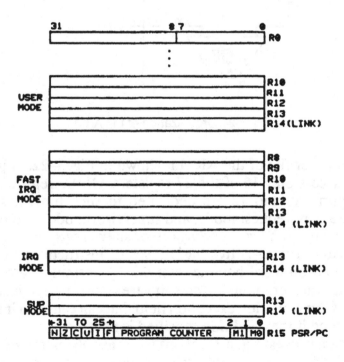

Fig. 3-22. Register file of the ARM

Most of the instructions in the ARM are executed in one clock cycle. The multiplication instructions execute, in the worst case, in 16 cycles. The actual time is a function of the value in the source registers.

The ARM supports only two addressing modes: program counter and base register relative. The ability to perform pre- and postindexing allows stacks and queues to be implemented in software easily.

Integraph Clipper

The Integraph Clipper originally was designed and produced by Fairchild Semiconductors, which Integraph subsequently bought. According to the manufacturer, the Clipper is a compromise between a CISC (complex-instruction-set computer) and a RISC.

The Clipper has 32 32-bit registers. It is hardwired with 101 instructions, which, by RISC standards, is slightly high, and has 67 high-level macroinstructions that operate on the basic data types. To simplify decoding, all instructions are formatted as multiples of 16-bit parcels. The most frequently used instructions are the shortest.

Each instruction specifies the operation to be performed and the type and location of the operands. Operands may reside in memory, in a register, or in the instruction itself. To increase the speed of decoding, all instructions contain from one to four 16-bit parcels. Figure 3-23 shows the instruction formats of the Clipper.

The Clipper instructions fall into two categories, those with addresses and those without addresses. The former are memory-reference instructions, and the latter are data-handling instructions that can execute generally in one cycle.

Although instructions may have zero, one, or two operands, only one operand can access a memory address. Thus, the instruction set consists of 10 functional categories: load/store, move, arithmetic, logical, shift/rotate, conversion (they convert single- or double-precision floating-point numbers into integers rounded to IEEE specifications), compare, string, stack, and control.

The Clipper provides nine memory-addressing modes, as shown

INSTRUCTION FORMATS – NO ADDRESS

REGISTER

```
15            8 7      4 3      0
| OPCODE        | R1   | R2    |
```

QUICK

```
15            8 7      4 3      0
| OPCODE        | QUICK | R2   |
```

16-BIT IMMEDIATE

```
15            8 7      4 3      0
| OPCODE        | 1 0 1 1 | R2 |
| S |   IMMEDIATE              |
31 30                        16
```

CONTROL

```
15              8 7            0
| OPCODE         | BYTE        |
```

MACRO

```
15          9 8 7 6            0
| OPCODE  P 0 0 0   CODE       |
| 0 0 0 0 0 0 0 |  R1  |  R2   |
31            24 23   20 19   16
```

32-BIT IMMEDIATE

```
15            8 7      4 3      0
| OPCODE        | 0 0 1 1 | R2 |
|      IMMEDIATE LOW          |
| S |   IMMEDIATE HIGH        |
47 46                        32
```

INSTRUCTION FORMATS – WITH ADDRESS

RELATIVE

```
15            8 7      4 3      0
| OPCODE      0 | R1   | R2    |
```

RELATIVE PLUS 12-BIT DISPLACEMENT

```
15            8 7      4 3      0
| OPCODE      1 1 0 1 0 | R1    |
| S | DISPLACEMENT      | R2    |
31 30                20 19     16
```

RELATIVE PLUS 32-BIT DISPLACEMENT

```
15            8 7      4 3      0
| OPCODE        | 0 1 1 0 | R1 |
| 0 0 0 0 0 0 0 0 0 0 0 0 | R2 |
|   DISPLACEMENT LOW         |
| S | DISPLACEMENT HIGH       |
63 62                       48
```

16-BIT ABSOLUTE

```
15            8 7      4 3      0
| OPCODE        | 1 1 0 1 1 | R2 |
| S |   ADDRESS                 |
31 30                        16
```

32-BIT ABSOLUTE

```
15            8 7      4 3      0
| OPCODE        | 0 0 1 1 | R2 |
|      ADDRESS LOW            |
| S |   ADDRESS HIGH          |
47 46                        32
```

PC-RELATIVE PLUS 16-BIT DISPLACEMENT

```
15            8 7      4 3      0
| OPCODE        | 1 1 0 0 1 | R2 |
| S |   DISPLACEMENT           |
31 32                        16
```

PC-RELATIVE PLUS 32-BIT DISPLACEMENT

```
15            8 7      4 3      0
| OPCODE        | 0 0 1 1 | R2 |
|   DISPLACEMENT LOW         |
| S | DISPLACEMENT HIGH       |
47 46                        32
```

RELATIVE INDEXED

```
15            8 7      4 3      0
| OPCODE        | 1 1 1 0 | R1 |
| 0 0 0 0 0 0 0 |  RX  |  R2   |
31            24 23   20 19   16
```

PC INDEXED

```
15            8 7      4 3      0
| OPCODE      1 1 1 0 1 0 0 0 0 |
| 0 0 0 0 0 0 0 |  RX  |  R2   |
31            24 23   20 19   16
```

Fig. 3-23. Instruction format of the Clipper

in Fig. 3–24, to specify a unique virtual address as the sum of several factors. In the relative mode and the two relative-with-displacement modes, a virtual address may be contained in a register or may be derived from the addition of the contents of a specified register and a displacement contained in the instruction.

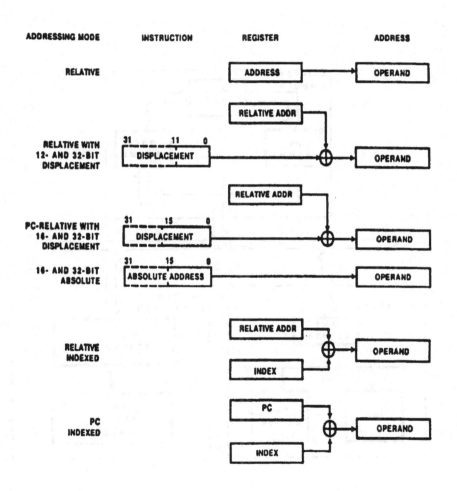

Fig. 3-24. Clipper addressing modes

The Clipper is, actually, a module that consists of three devices mounted on a printed circuit board: the integer/floating-point processor, the instruction cache/memory-management unit, and the data cache/memory-management unit. A typical Clipper-based system is shown in Fig. 3–25. A more detailed diagram of the processor appears in Fig. 3–26.

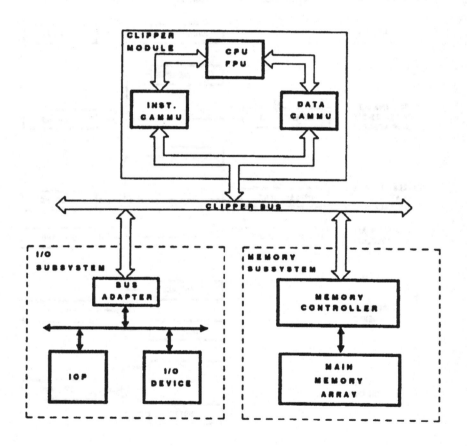

Fig. 3-25. Clipper-based system

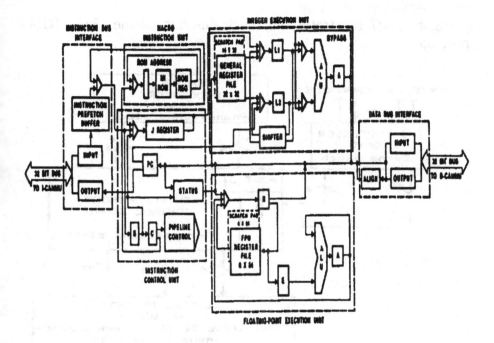

Fig. 3-26. Internal structure of the Clipper processor

Gallium Arsenide RISC Processor

In late 1984, Texas Instruments and Control Data Corporation undertook a joint project, under the sponsorship of the Defense Advanced Research Projects Agency (DARPA). The project involved the design and production of a RISC processor using gallium arsenide (GaAs), the fastest semiconductor material. This section describes the methodology followed during the design and production stages of this processor.

The designers decided that a maximum gate count of 10,000 was necessary to include all of the important functions on the processor. Actually, this RISC processor consists of different devices that accommodate the processor, the floating-point coprocessor, and the memory-management unit.

Figure 3–27 illustrates the block diagram of the GaAs RISC processor.

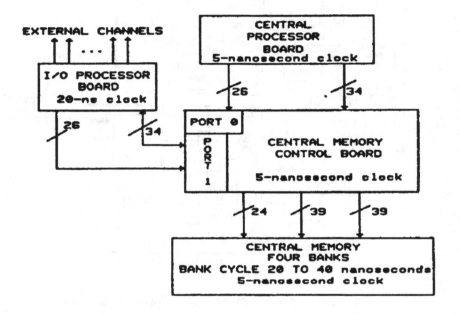

Fig. 3-27. Block diagram of the GaAs RISC processor

The system has full 32-bit data paths throughout and supports 64 megabytes of virtual and real address space. The objective of the system is to operate at a speed of 5 nanoseconds, thereby attaining a peak execution rate of 200 million instructions per second. All elements in the system operate from the same clock system.

The processor is the heart of the system, generating all memory addresses for both instructions and operands, but the other two devices also are capable of executing their own specific instructions, through a common instruction bus. Each device controls a six-level pipeline, so an orderly exit and return can be taken for an interrupt routine. The memory-management unit supports a fully segmented and paged virtual memory system. This device also controls independent instruction and data caches, both operating in parallel. The i/o processor and the central processor boards have separate ports on the central memory control, or CMC, board to a multibank central memory, thus minimizing contention and conflict delays.

The central processor board consists of a processor device, a floating-point coprocessor, two memory-management units, two processor board interface devices, and several RAM and support devices used as cache memory.

The GaAs processor system was designed initially with a four-level pipeline, to achieve fetching of an instruction in one cycle. The cache memory, however, could not support the requisite 5-ns memory cycle. On the other hand, a pipelined memory preserved the 5-ns cycle time, by permitting the memory to be accessed over two cycles. The designers decided to have a six-level pipeline: Instruction Fetch cycle I (I1), Instruction Fetch cycle II (I2), ALU Execute (EX), Memory Access Cycle I (M1), Memory Access Cycle II (M2), and Write Register File (WR).

The nonmemory access pipestages EX and WR execute an instruction and write the register file. The memory pipestages I1, I2, M1, and M2 place the memory address out during the I1 or M1 cycle and latch the returning instruction or operand data during I2 and M2. The memory chips have pipeline registers integrated on-chip, with the memory array to support pipelined access. The pipelined memory access increased the complexity of the design, but decreased the cycle time by 39%.

The GaAs processor system has some hardware pipeline interlocks. Data dependencies between register-to-register instructions are resolved in hardware, as shown in Fig. 3–28.

```
ADD, R0, R1, R2      R2=R1+R0    I1   I2   EX  M1   M2   WR
SUB, R2, R3, R4      R4=R2-R3         I1   I2  EX   M1   M2   WR
```

Although the ADD does not write R2 until the WR
pipestage, the hardware shortstopping logic provides
the sum of R1 and R0 to the SUB instruction in its
EX pipestage.

Fig. 3-28. Data dependencies in the GaAs processor

Software shedules instructions after a branch, as shown in Fig. 3–29. The software must ensure that instructions left in the pipeline after a branch do not depend upon its destination. If no benign instruction can be found to fit into the delay slot, then the pipeline must be filled with a no-operation instruction.

```
0000   BRC,GT,0F000   I1   I2   EX   M1   M2   WR
0001   NOP                 I1   I2   EX   M1   M2   WR
0002   NOP                      I1   I2   EX   M1   M2   WR
F000   ADD                           I1   I2   EX   M1   M2   WR
```

The branch delay for a six-stage pipeline is two.
The two instructions after a branch are always executed since these instructions are already in the
pipeline when the branch is evaluated during EX.

Fig. 3-29. Branch delays in the GaAs processor

The central processor, whose data path is shown in Fig. 3–30, has a dedicated bus for operand and instruction memory fetches. The memory interface consists of a 24-bit-wide instruction address bus, a 32-bit-wide instruction data bus, a 26-bit-wide operand address bus, and a 32-bit-wide operand data bus. Instructions are word-addressed. Operands are byte-addressed. Operand data may be in byte, halfword, or word format. The control interface provides status, memory read/write control, and interrupt information to the system or the central processing unit.

The CPU execution model – read two operands, perform an ALU operation, write the result – is supported by a 32-bit-wide data path. The major elements of the data path are the register file, the temporary registers, the ALU, the Program Status Register, and the program counters.

An instruction is fetched using the address in PCNXT during I1 and I2. During EX, the register file is read onto the a and b buses. Alternatively, the contents of result1, result2, or result3 may be "shortstopped" to one or both buses. The ALU performs the arithmetic, logical, or shift operations. A result from these operations is latched by the result1 register on ALU and memory instructions, sent to the PCNXT on control transfer instructions, or latched by the Processor Status Register (PSW) on an implicit move to the PSW instruction. During M1, the result1 contents are sent to the result2 register. The result1 contents may be used as an address for an operand cache access. The condition codes, if set by an instruction, are evaluated during M1 and latched in the PSW. During M2, the result3 register latches the ALU output, the result2 contents, or the memory interface.

During WR, the register file is written by the result3 register. During each pipestage, the instruction address is passed from one program counter to the next. Therefore, PCNXT, PCP1, PC, PCM1, and PCLST hold the addresses of the instructions in the I1, I2, EX, M1, and M2 pipestages, respectively.

Since floating-point operations cannot be executed in one cycle, even with such a fast semiconductor as GaAs, a separate floating-

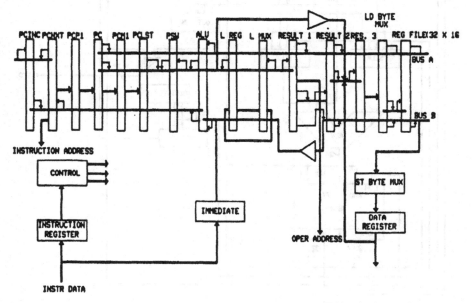

Fig. 3-30. Central processing unit data path

point coprocessor executes the floating-point instructions of the GaAs instruction set. The coprocessor also contains hardware support for fast integer multiplication and division.

The data path of the floating-point coprocessor consists of the following major elements, shown in Fig. 3–31: a 4 x 64-bit register file, an exponent control, a 64-bit shift unit, a 34-bit arithmetic unit, and a processor status register.

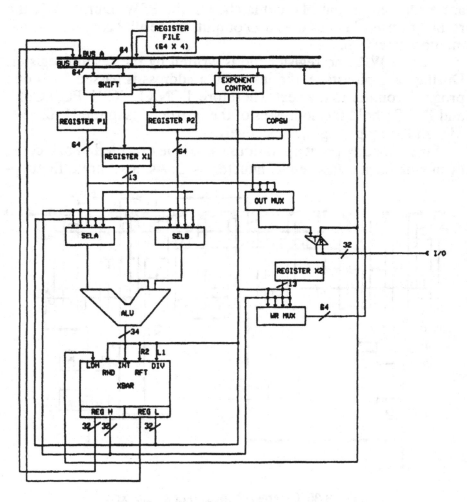

Fig. 3-31. Floating-point coprocessor data path

Floating-point operations require a more complex execution model than their integer counterparts. The floating-point coprocessor is used iteratively to perform the various parts of a floating-point operation. For example, a double-precision floating-point addition begins by reading the two operands out of the register file during the EX pipestage. The exponents of these operands are compared, and the appropriate shift amount is sent to the shifter for denormalization. The shifter denormalizes the mantissa with the smaller exponent.

The preliminary result exponent is latched in the X1 register and the mantissas in the P1 and P2 registers. During the M1 pipestage, the arithmetic unit adds the low parts of the two mantissas. The carry-out is saved and used during M2 to add the upper parts of the two mantissas. The next instruction converts the lower part of the arithmetic unit's 2s complement output to sign magnitude. The next instruction uses the arithmetic unit in the M2 pipestage to convert the upper part of the result mantissa to sign magnitude form. The sign magnitude mantissa is normalized in the next instruction during the M1 pipestage. During M2, the low part of the mantissa is rounded. The final instruction uses the arithmetic unit during the M2 pipestage to round the upper part of the normalized mantissa, reformat the result into double-precision format with the exponent, and write that result into the register file. The floating-point condition codes in the PSW are updated in different pipestages, depending on whether they are the result of a shift or add operation.

The floating-point coprocessor cannot issue an instruction during every cycle due to resource conflicts between instructions. These instruction cycles must be filled with no-operation instructions if no other useful instructions can be scheduled. These no-op slots provide an opportunity for the execution of central processor or memory-management unit instructions in parallel with the floating-point coprocessor operation. A translator/reorganizer schedules these operations so that the GaAs processor system may achieve maximum parallelism.

WRITABLE-INSTRUCTION-SET COMPUTER (WISC)

Description of representative RISC processors, covering the extremes of the RISC concept from the original Berkeley RISC to the Clipper, is intended to provide the reader with adequate information to draw conclusions about the advantages and disadvantages of RISC.

The RISC concept has been the subject of a fair amount of controversy. As an example, in the April 1987 issue of *BYTE*, Phil Koopman examined the RISC concept, revealed facts that limit RISC's favor with some, and proposed a new architecture — the writable-instruction-set computer. Koopman investigated some RISC weaknesses and proposed corrections in his concept.

RISC devices execute most instructions in one clock cycle. The real resource limitation is the amount of time required to reference program memory. In the WISC approach, the use of as much of the memory bandwidth as possible is a desirable feature.

Koopman does not agree with the RISC rule that the control unit must be hardwired. Since a designer can make a small amount of microcode memory extremely fast in relation to large amounts of program memory, while achieving a reasonable cost-performance tradeoff, Koopman sees no reason that a microcoded processor cannot achieve single-memory-reference-cycle operation for most of its instructions.

Next, Koopman finds problems, mainly in restricted performance, with the limited instruction set of a RISC. He claims that, if a processor can support additional instructions without loss of execution speed, then the requirement of a reduced instruction set is no longer realistic. So, he states, a WISC architecture should not restrict the number and type of instructions unnecessarily. Koopman also disagrees with the restriction of load/store instructions as the only memory-reference instructions. He agrees that such instructions reduce clock-cycle times, but, if virtual memory is not being used or if a memory reference can be combined with another operation, then the load/store restriction also becomes unnecessary.

Koopman favors a fixed-length instruction format but recommends a simple architecture that should not need sophisticated optimizing compilers.

A major drawback in RISC architectures, in Koopman's estimation, is that the low semantic content of each instruction requires a high memory bandwidth, resulting in a sharp memory price-performance tradeoff. His concept minimizes the number of memory references. Furthermore, WISC goals should be to execute all instructions in a single clock memory-reference cycle and to use 100% of the available memory bandwidth, unless, for a particular application or high-level language run-time environment, a microcoded complex instruction clearly results in performance superior to multiple simple instructions. Naturally, instructions that involve memory operand accesses will be longer than a single memory cycle but will nonetheless tend to keep the memory productively engaged at all times.

Finally, Koopman recommends the presence of a hardware-implemented, push-down, last-in/first-out stack. He proposes the use of two separate stacks, one for storage of subroutine return addresses and the other for data storage. The advantage of the first stack is that returns can be processed at a fast rate. The use of a data stack simplifies the machine's operation and increases its speed by eliminating the need for operand decoding. Since a stack machine implicitly addresses certain elements on the stack relative to the current stack pointer position, the CPU does not suffer any delays while source and destination registers are selected from a large register bank. Furthermore, the instruction bits freed by not needing fields for selection of registers allow the use of a narrow word size (16 bits or less), the packing of multiple opcodes into each program word, or the use of constants or other values in the same word as an opcode, all while maintaining a simple instruction format.

After description of likes and dislikes about the RISC concept and the RISC/CISC advantages to be applied to the WISC concept, Koopman proposes the block diagram of a WISC architecture shown in Fig. 3–32. This architecture (to this point, still a paper design) employs a data stack, an ALU with a small number of registers (perhaps only one), a return stack with a bidirectional data path to the program counter for subroutine-call address manipulation, a program memory, and a microcoded controller. All of the resources are connected to a central data bus, with access to i/o services through an appropriate interface.

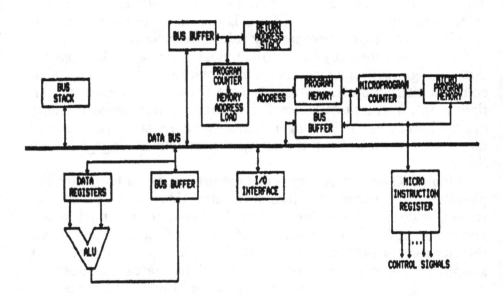

Fig. 3-32. Proposed architecture of WISC

Koopman reveals some additional interesting features about his WISC concept. The registers above the ALU can hold the top one or two data-stack elements. These registers allow use of a single-ported, data-stack RAM.

The entire instruction decoding path, from the return-address stack up to and including the microinstruction register, is completely independent of the main data bus. This independence allows ALU and data-stack operations on data while instructions are fetched and decoded simultaneously. This arrangement permits use of nearly 100% of the memory bandwidth. An additional benefit of this scheme is that an instruction prefetch unit and queue are unnecessary.

The microinstruction register forms a single-level pipeline, thus eliminating wasted time that otherwise would result from waiting for microprogram memory access in a nonpipelined design. This scheme, however, adds to the instruction access time – a minimum of two microcycles are required for all opcodes.

Another disadvantage of this scheme is that delayed microinstruction branches must be used for condition code testing. This problem, however, can be avoided by the application of the small high-speed memory used to implement the microprogram memory and data-stack memory. This type of memory should allow for multiple microcode cycles within each memory-cycle time, essentially eliminating the impact of these drawbacks on system performance.

VERY-LONG-INSTRUCTION-WORD COMPUTER (VLIW)

Philosophy

The very-long-instruction-word principle is based on multiplicity of events and processors. Thus, if one processor is fast, two are faster, and n are very much faster. Practical implementation of this approach calls for one big processor with n ALUs connected to the same register file. The name *Very Long Instruction Word* is derived from the fact that each of these n ALUs would need to be told what to do and, consequently, the instruction word would need to be n times longer. As all of the processors would work with one set of registers, communication overhead would be practically nonexistent.

The idea of VLIW resulted from the research of Yale professor Josh Fisher and several of his graduate students. One of these students, John R. Ellis, wrote an extensive dissertation describing VLIW and a compiler called Bulldog. Peter Wayner, a graduate student at Cornell, has contributed to the design of yet another VLIW compiler to be used by IBM.

The basic idea of VLIW is a technique called *trace scheduling*. Trace scheduling assumes that a computer spends its time executing one particular path, or trace, through a program. These traces contain much more parallelism than basic blocks of a program. The compiler picks a trace, generates a machine code for the trace, and replaces the trace with the machine code. The compiler then repeats the process until the entire flow graph of a program is translated into machine code. Estimates of execution frequency guide the compiler in picking traces. The blocks most likely to be executed comprise the first trace, those likely to be executed next comprise the second trace, and so on. Figure 3–33 illustrates the flow graph of a simple program and the traces selected from it.

Occasionally, a computer using a VLIW compiler may follow one branch off the path, but a programmer hopes that, with the use of so-called trace scheduling, the process will return soon. Once the compiler picks a trace, it compacts the code along the trace and moves all operations that can be performed simultaneously into the same instruction.

Compiling a program for a VLIW machine is a matter of guessing the right path before a program executes. Bulldog uses loop nesting and programmer-supplied hints to make reasonable guesses about block execution frequency. This method appears to work fairly well without too much help from a programmer.

For various reasons, a trace never extends past a loop boundary. That is, a trace can include only blocks from the same loop, but no blocks from containing or contained loops.

The underlying premises of trace scheduling are that the most likely execution paths through a program can be predicted at compile time and that most of the execution time is spent in those paths. For most scientific programs, these are valid assumptions. The time-critical control structures of scientific code tend to be quite simple and highly predictable, consisting mainly of nested loops with a few conditionals that usually branch one way most of the time. Clearly, these premises are less likely to be true for system programs.

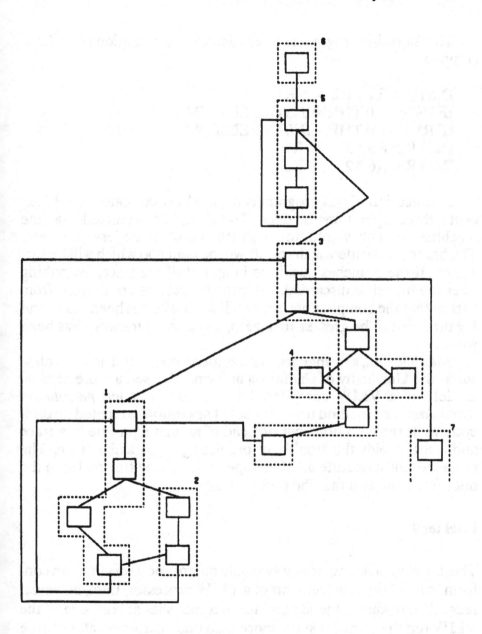

Fig. 3-33. Traces in a flow path

The following program segment depicts the operation of a VLIW compiler:

INSTR1: R1 + R2 — > R1;
IF R9 < = 0 THEN INSTR2 ELSE R4 + R5 — >;
IF R8 < = 0 THEN INSTR3 ELSE R7 * 2 — > R7
INSTR2: R3 * 2 — > R3
INSTR3: R6 * 2 — > R6

In execution of this program code, a VLIW computer would execute three operations at once. The compiler predicted that the machine probably would find both R8 and R9 to be less than zero. The branches decide which results will be kept and which will be forgotten. If the branches decide to jump out of the trace, everything after the branch is discarded. All three operations are derived from a trace that the compiler has chosen. If a mistake has been made and R9 turns out to be greater than zero, all of the extra work has been wasted.

Alex Nicolau, a former graduate student of Fish and now a professor at the University of California at Irvine, devised a more general model for a VLIW compiler. His method is called *percolation scheduling*. The method treats the set of operations executed on each cycle as a tree with branches, instead of as a straight line in a trace and, thus, avoids the trouble of predicting a particular trace. The processor must execute all of the operations in the tree and save the ones from the path that the process takes.

Intel i860

There are not many currently available microprocessors that can conform to all of the requirements of a VLIW processor. Intel, however, recently introduced the i860, which accomplishes at least one of the VLIW requirements. It starts more than one instruction at the same time. The i860 is a rather sophisticated and powerful processor. Intel calls the i860 "Cray on a chip."

The block diagram of this processor is in Fig. 3–34. The processor consists of nine units: a core execution unit, a floating-point control unit, a floating-point adder unit, a floating-point multiplier unit, a graphics unit, a paging unit, an instruction cache, a data cache, and a bus and cache control.

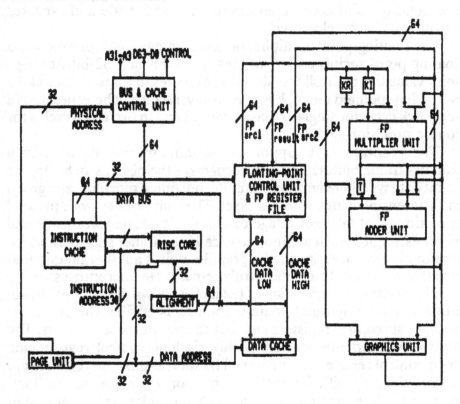

Fig. 3-34. Block diagram of the Intel i860

The core unit controls the operation of the entire system. The unit executes load, store, integer, bit, and control-transfer instructions; it also fetches instructions for the floating-point unit. The core unit is equipped with 32 32-bit, general-purpose registers for the manipulation of integer data.

The floating-point unit uses a separate set of registers that can be accessed either as 16 64-bit registers or as 32 32-bit registers. Special load and store instructions also access these same registers as 8 128-bit registers.

The floating-point adder performs addition, subtraction, comparison, and conversion on 64-bit and 32-bit floating-point values. The floating-point adder operates in pipelined mode and executes instructions in one clock cycle.

The floating-point multiplier performs integer multiplication and floating-point reciprocal operations on 64-bit and 32-bit floating-point values. A multiplier instruction executes in three to four clock cycles. In pipelined mode, however, a new result can be generated in one clock cycle for single-precision values and in two clock cycles for double-precision values.

The graphics unit supports three-dimensional drawing in a graphics frame buffer. This unit recognizes the pixel as an 8-, 16-, or 32-bit data type. The unit can compute individual red, blue, and green color intensity values within a pixel. The unit does so with parallel operations that take advantage of the 64-bit internal word size and 64-bit external bus. In addition to excellent parallel features and exceptional computing speed, the graphics unit is another unique feature that make the Intel i860 a truly remarkable microprocessor.

The register configuration of the i860 is shown in Fig. 3–35. In addition to the integer and floating-point register files, the processor contains six control registers and four special-purpose registers. The control registers are accessible only via load-control register and store-control register instructions. The special-purpose registers are used by a few specific instructions, three of which are used in floating-point operations and initiate both an adder and a multiplier operation. Only the vector-integer instructions use the MERGE register, which accumulates the results of multiple addition operations used in graphics.

The i860 addresses memory in byte units with a paged virtual-address space of 2^{32} bytes. Data and instructions can reside at any memory location. Normally, multibyte data values are stored in memory in little-endian format — i.e., with the least significant byte at the lowest memory address, as shown in Fig. 3–36. As an option that may be dynamically selected by software when the processor is in supervisor mode, the i860 also accepts the big-endian mode — i.e., the most significant byte of a datum resides in the lowest address.

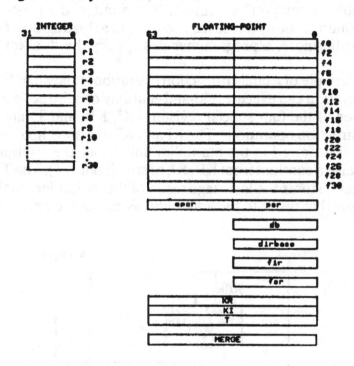

Fig. 3-35. Register configuration of the i860

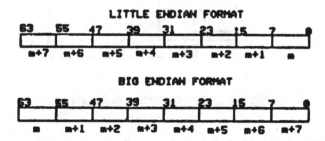

Fig. 3-36. Little-endian and big-endian format

The i860 accesses 4K byte, fixed-size page frames of contiguous addresses in main memory.

The i860 achieves its execution sophistication by pipelining and by "double-instruction" execution. In the latter, the processor executes simultaneously a core instruction and a floating-point instruction. Furthermore, a programmer can specify the dual-instruction mode.

An example of a dual-instruction operation is shown in Fig. 3–37. This operation can execute add-and-multiply or subtract-and-multiply. Three of the four special registers (KI, KR, and T) are used in dual-instruction operations. The KI and KR registers hold constants that are transferred to the multiplier unit. Thus, the multiplier unit may receive a constant from KR, KI, or src1 (Source 1). The T (Transfer) register stores the last-stage result of the multiplier pipeline and can supply that result to the adder unit as one of the operands.

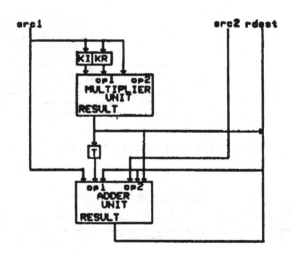

Fig. 3-37. Dual-operation data path

A four-bit field in the opcode controls the data path of the operands — i.e., it dictates whether an operand is to be transferred from KR, KI, src1, or src2.

SUMMARY

Several advanced microprocessors are discussed in this chapter, each matching various new computer architecture principles, such as RISC and VLIW. Other advanced microprocessors fall into these categories but are not mentioned in this chapter, because description of their architecture would be merely repetitive. Two microprocessors that are somewhat more novel in architecture and instruction set, the Am29000 and the INMOS transputer, have been singled out for treatment in later chapters because of the detail required to do them justice.

NOTES

[1] Cray Research, *CRAY-1 Optimization Guide*

[2] John L. Hennessy et al., "The MIPS Machine," *COMPCON*, I.E.E.E. (Spring 1982)

[3] Anant Agarwal et al., "On-chip Instruction Caches for High Performance Processors," *Proceedings,* Stanford Conference on Advanced Research in VLSI (March 1987)

[4] John L. Hennessy et al., "Hardware/Software Tradeoffs for Increased Performance," *Proceedings,* SIGARCH/SIGPLAN (Palto Alto: March 1982)

[5] Robert Colwell el al., "Instructions Sets and Beyond: Computers, Complexity, and Controversy," *Computer* (September 1985)

[6] H. Azaria and D. Tabak, "The MODHEL Microcomputer for RISCs Study," *Microprocessing and Microprogramming*, 12, Nos. 3-4 (October-November 1983)

[7] D. A. Patterson and C. H. Sequin, "A VLSI RISC," *Computer,* 15, No. 9 (September 1982)

[8] M. Hopkins, "Definition of RISC," *Proceedings of the Conference on High Level Language Architecture* (Los Angeles, CA: May 1984)

[9] *Am29000 32-bit Streamlined Instruction Processor*, Advanced Micro Devices (Sunnyvale, CA: 1988)

[10] R. Jenkins and R. Moore, "Computer Architecture," (Baltimore, MD: The Johns Hopkins University Whiting School of Engineering)

Chapter 4
Data-Flow Computers

CONCEPT BEHIND DATA FLOW

All of the advanced microprocessors discussed in the preceding chapters are von Neumann-type. A program is executed in a sequence of ordered operations that a programmer specifies. A program counter points to the memory locations in which these operations and their operands reside, and the processor's control unit generates the appropriate control signals to activate within the processor those components that eventually will execute a particular operation. Due to this "controlled" flow of instructions and data, this type of processor sometimes is referred to as a *control-flow* processor. Remember, however, that, notwithstanding the sequential execution by a control-flow processor, it can display various forms of parallelism. Consider, for example, the i860, whose floating-point unit can execute various processes between the adder and multiplier units. Although these processes are sequential in nature, they can be executed in parallel and can transmit data to or receive data from each other. See also the discussion of the transputer in Chapter 6.

The term *data flow* has been coined to refer to systems that do not have a centralized control unit and program counter but, rather, select operations for execution when their operands have been computed. In this sense, the flow of data between operations provides the sequencing control that a program counter normally provides in a conventional control-flow processor.

Since the operands of several "actors" (functions or operators) may be available simultaneously, the data-flow approach also facilitates the exploitation of parallelism in a program.

Two types of data-flow operations are defined. In a data-driven type, operations are executed in an order determined by the availability of input data. In a demand-driven type, operations are executed in an order determined by the requirements for data.

A data-flow program may be represented in the form of a directed graph in which the nodes represent "actors" and the arcs show the data dependencies between actors. For example, the addition of two values may be represented by the actor in Fig. 4–1a.

An operation is carried out according to *firing rules* – a term that should be known to those familiar with Petri Nets. Tokens are placed on, or removed from, the arcs. When an operation is completed, the arc has "fired," and a token is placed on the output arc of the actor. The placement of input and output tokens may be seen in Fig. 4–1b and c. For an actor to fire, tokens must be absent from the output arcs of the actor.

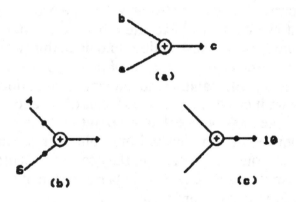

Fig. 4-1. Directed graph form of a data-flow program

Two other symbols that are used in data-flow programs are the *switch* and the *merge*. These symbols, shown in Fig. 4–2a and b, appear similar, except that the true-false result acts as input to a switch and output from a merge. Both of these symbols are control functions and are similar to a decision diamond in a control-flow program. In fact, since data-flow symbols are not yet standardized, some data-flow programmers prefer to depict a switch as the control-flow decision diamond. See Fig. 4–2c. Another way to illustrate the merge is shown in Fig. 4–2d.

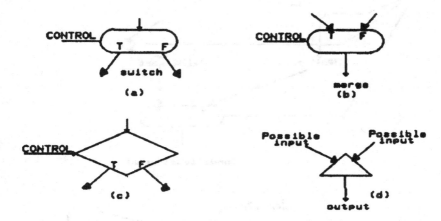

Fig. 4-2. Merge and switch symbols in a data-flow program

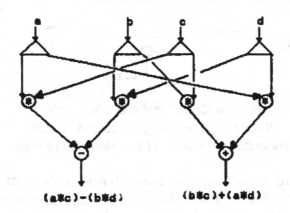

Fig. 4-3. Program graph

Figure 4–3 shows that actors may be connected into a program graph. Conditional and loop graphs may be formed as demonstrated in Fig. 4–4. Figure 4–4 highlights that cyclic graphs are allowed, that multiple tokens may be passed between operations, and that execution is data-driven.

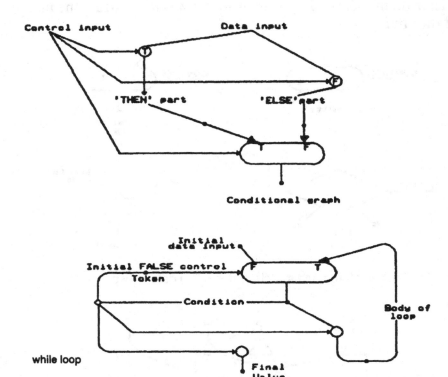

Fig. 4-4. Conditional and loop graphs
(*Data Flow Computing*, by John A. Sharp)
By written permission of Ellis Harwood Limited

With regard to cyclic graphs, John Sharp lists two potential weaknesses [1]. The first is a so-called deadly embrace, which Fig. 4-5 depicts. This problem may be eliminated by the use of only switches and merges.

The second problem is the "race condition," shown in Fig. 4-6. If the graph in Fig. 4-6 were within the body of a loop, $X1$ and $X2$ normally would be inputted into the program and, depending on the condition C (conditionals and iteration are discussed later in this chapter), $X1$ and $X2$ would be matched with $Y1$ and $Y2$, respectively. Now assume that $X1$ is routed through program segment A, which is a long one, while $X2$ is routed through the shorter program segment B. As $X2$ takes less time, it "races" to C first and creates a matching problem, because $X2$ now is matched with $Y1$ rather than $Y2$. The program may be corrected if labels or colors are attached to tokens to ensure that only tokens with the same labels or colors can be combined in a computation.

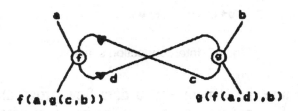

Fig. 4-5. A "deadly embrace" in a data-flow program

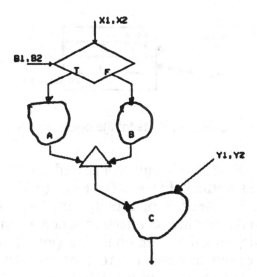

Fig. 4-6. A "race" in a data-flow program

The deadly embrace shown in Fig. 4–5 should not be confused with the interconnection schema of data-flow programs. Such a schema, which, incidentally, is legal, is shown in Fig. 4–7.

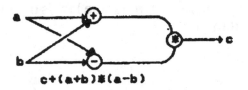

c+(a+b)*(a-b)

Fig. 4-7. Interconnection schema

Now examine the structure of a data-flow program in greater detail. A data-flow program consists of "activity templates." The activity template in Fig. 4–8 shows four "fields." One field denotes the operation to be carried out (opcode). Two fields, each containing one operand, are called *receivers*. One field is for the destination of the result.

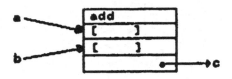

Fig. 4-8. Activity fields for the operation a + b = c

Activity templates can be interconnected to form a program. The interconnected schema in Fig. 4–7 $((a+b) * (a-b) = c)$ is arranged, in Fig. 4–9, as a collection of activity templates. In the first two templates, observe the interconnection schema from Fig. 4–7. The last template denotes the main operation (multiplication of a sum and a difference) and the destination of the result. Thus, this template may be called the *instruction* of the data-flow program segment. An instruction is the fixed portion of an activity template and contains the operation code and the destination or destinations of a result.

Each destination field specifies a target receiver, by providing the "address" of some activity template and an "input integer" that specifies which of the receivers in the template is the target.

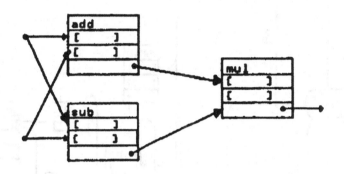

Fig. 4-9. Interconnection of activity templates

The switch and merge actors are used in the manipulation of conditional statements. The switch in Fig. 4-6 is labeled as (T)rue and (F)alse. The merge actor simply forwards to the next step in the program the datum that results from the condition.

A conditional statement example, given by Dennis [2], is shown in Fig. 4-10. The statement is:

$y: = (if\, x\, >3\, then\, x\, +\, 2\, else\, x\, -1)\, *\, 4.$

The control input $(x >3)$ is evaluated at the switch as being either true or false. The evaluated condition follows the appropriate route and ends at the merge actor.

The iterative schema of a data-flow program is shown in Fig. 4-11.

A point to be noted in the activity templates is the opcode field. This field does not always denote instructions in the pure sense of the word — e.g., add or multiply. It may denote an action such as "switch" or "greater." Thus, in addition to denoting a primitive function, a data-flow actor may denote a function such as "copy" or "apply." The former can be used to carry out the same primitive function at two

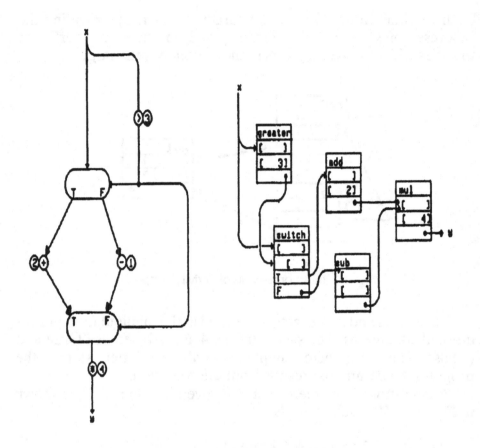

Fig. 4-10. Conditional schema and its activity templates
(*The Varieties of Data-Flow Computers,* by Jack Dennis)

different nodes of the graph — i.e., to carry out a duplicating action. The "apply" function may be used to represent an application of a user-defined function. An example in which the "copy" and "apply" functions are used appears in Fig. 4–12, which represents an algorithm for the calculation of factorials.

As stated previously, the use of symbols varies among authors and designers. For example, the factorial algorithm in Fig. 4–12 is represented in a slightly different format in Fig. 4–13. In this diagram, actors are represented by rectangles.

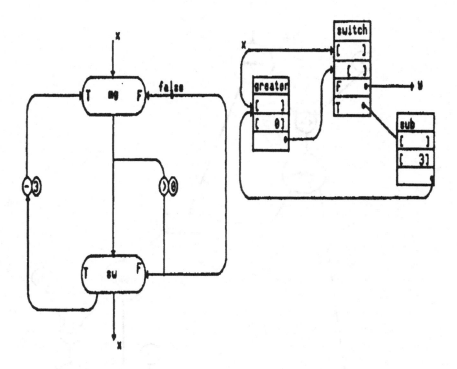

Fig. 4-11. Iteration schema and its activity templates
(*The Varieties of Data-Flow Computers,* by Jack Dennis)

An activity template is activated when there is an operand present in each receiver. In such a case, the contents of the template form an "operation packet" that contains the opcode, the operands, and the destinations. An operation packet specifies one "result packet" that contains a value (the result) and a destination for each destination field in a particular activity template. Upon generation of a result packet, the value (result) is placed in the activity template receiver that the destination field of the result packet has designated.

Dennis views the basic execution mechanism for instructions in a data-flow program in the manner shown in Fig. 4–14.

The activity store contains a collection of a program's activity templates. Each template resides at a particular address, which is entered in a first-in-first-out buffer, the instruction queue, when an

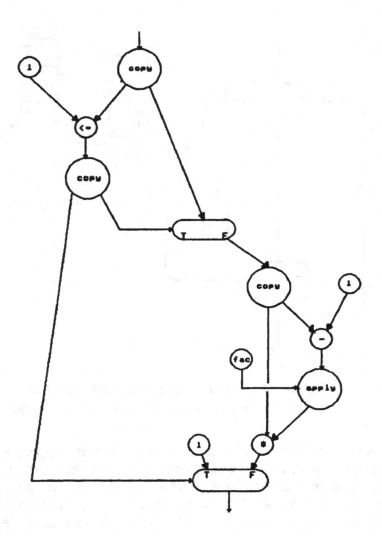

function Factorial (n:Integer);Integer;
begin
   if n < = 1 then Factorial : = 1
   else Factorial :n * Factorial (n-1)
end

Fig. 4-12. Data-flow program for calculation of factorials

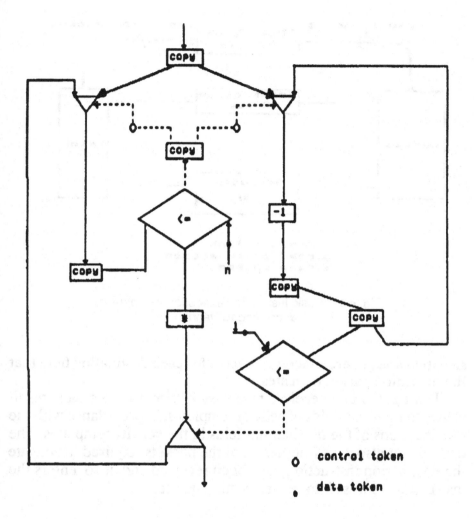

Fig. 4-13. Variation of the factorial algorithm data flow

instruction is ready to be executed.

The fetch unit takes an instruction address from the instruction queue and fetches the activity template contained in the activity store at the address. The fetch unit forms the activity template into an operation packet and passes it onto the operation unit.

The operation unit executes the operation that the opcode has

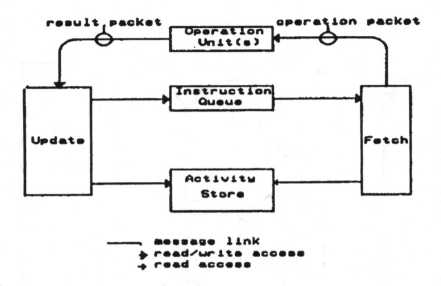

Fig. 4-14. Basic instruction execution mechanism
according to Dennis

specified and generates a result packet for each destination field that the operation packet indicates.

The update unit receives result packets and routes their result values to operand fields of activity templates, in accordance with the specifications of the destination fields in the activity templates. The update unit also tests whether all of the packets required to activate the destination instruction have been received and, if so, enters the instruction address into the instruction queue.

EXAMPLES OF DATA-FLOW COMPUTERS

Srini [3] presents seven data-flow architecture proposals, which are described in this section. Approximately the same number and type of data-flow architectures are presented in other publications [4–6].

To date, data-flow computers are classified in two general categories: static and dynamic.

A static data-flow computer loads into memory the nodes of a program graph, before commencement of program execution. In this type of computer, one instance of a node at most is enabled for firing at any given time.

A dynamic data-flow computer displays a degree of parallelism by firing several instances of a node at any given time. For example, when a loop body in a program is represented as a node, a dynamic data-flow computer unfolds the loop at run time, by creating multiple instances of the node that represents the loop body, and attempts to execute these instances concurrently.

The only data-flow computer in microprocessor form has been the Japanese NEC PD7281 Image Pipelined Processor.

Static Data-Flow Computers

Among the data-flow proposals that Srini describes is a proposal originating at MIT. As of the date of Srini's article, MIT had not built a prototype machine of the data-flow computer, but its design had been used as the foundation for other prototypes, such as Texas Instruments' data-driven processor and the LAU processor.

Geffin [7] has proposed a data-flow system as a robot arm controller, using 1834 transputer microprocessors. This project has been carried out in simulation, but only a small prototype was built.

The MIT Computer. The basic building blocks of the MIT static data-flow computer are shown in Fig. 4–15. A more general diagram of the MIT computer is illustrated in Fig. 4–16.

The system consists of memory blocks, called *cell blocks*, that hold the opcode, operands, and addresses of destinations. A program to be executed is loaded into memory via a host computer, which some call *front-end*. In Fig. 4–15, the rectangles marked R1 and R2 are routing networks; R2 routes enabled instructions from memory to the processing elements (marked PE). Any generated results are transferred back to memory via R1. As stated previously, these

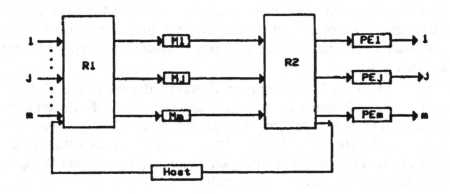

Fig. 4-15. Basic MIT static data-flow computer

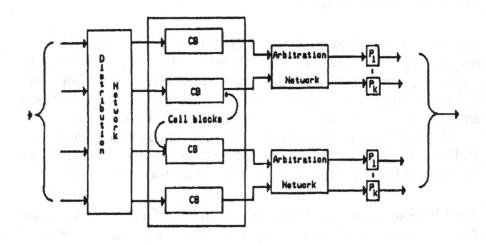

Fig. 4-16. More general diagram of the MIT computer

results are transferred as data packets, whose format is shown in Fig. 4–17.

An instruction token is enabled when the enabling count (EC) in Fig. 4–17 is identical to the concatenation of OPR and AKR.

31

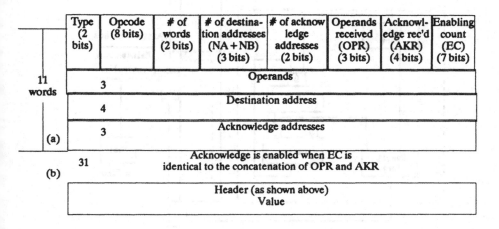

Type (2 bits)	Opcode (8 bits)	# of words (2 bits)	# of destination addresses (NA + NB) (3 bits)	# of acknowledge addresses (2 bits)	Operands received (OPR) (3 bits)	Acknowledge rec'd (AKR) (4 bits)	Enabling count (EC) (7 bits)

3	Operands
4	Destination address
3	Acknowledge addresses

(a)

Acknowledge is enabled when EC is identical to the concatenation of OPR and AKR

(b)   31

| Header (as shown above) |
| Value |

11 words

Fig. 4-17. Instruction (a) and data tokens (b) used by the MIT computer

Texas Instruments' Data-Driven Processor (DDP). The DDP, whose block diagram appears in Fig. 4–18, has been built, by the Equipment Group of TI at Austin, Texas, as a prototype with four processors.

The DDP executes Fortran programs loaded via a host processor. The instruction format is illustrated in Fig. 4–19.

A node is enabled when the predecessor count reaches zero. The enabled node is executed in the arithmetic-logic unit of the processing element. A result is routed to successor nodes in the processor's memory or another processing element. Communication among processing elements is carried out via the E-bus interconnection network as a series of 34-bit packets. Due to this type of token forwarding, more than one node may be enabled. Since a processing element has only a single ALU, enabled nodes are linked together in a queue, called the *pending instruction queue*. The top node in the queue is the one to be executed.

The DDP is equipped with a second bus, separate from the E bus, called the *maintenance bus*. This bus is present in each processing

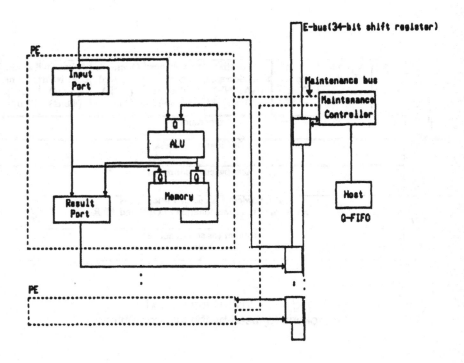

Fig. 4-18. Texas Instruments' DDP

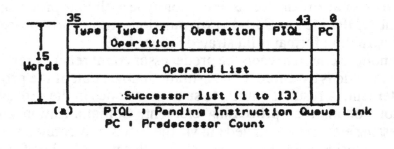

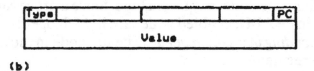

Fig. 4-19. Instruction format of the DDP

element and is used for transfers to and from memory, for monitoring of the performance of the processor, and for fault diagnostics.

The LAU Data-Flow Computer. This computer, whose block diagram is illustrated in Fig. 4–20, executes programs written in what its designers call a *single-assignment language*. Such programs are compiled to produce data-flow graphs in the host computer.

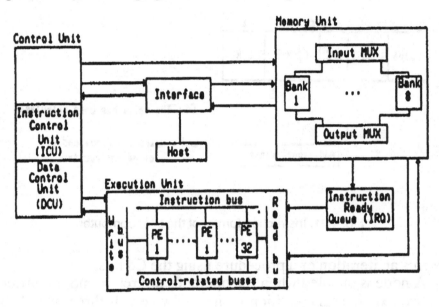

Fig. 4-20. The LAU data-flow computer

The instruction format of the LAU computer is shown in Fig. 4–21. An instruction, which consists of an operation part and a control part, is routed to two different points. The operation part is loaded into the memory, while the control part is transferred to the control unit.

The control unit of the LAU computer likewise consists of two parts: an instruction control unit (ICU) and a data control unit (DCU). It is the latter that enforces the single-assignment rule for data structures and detects termination for a task-level node that rep-

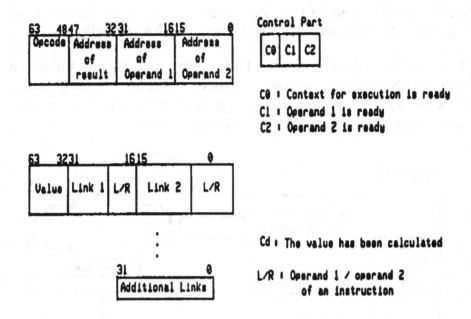

Fig. 4-21. Instruction format of the LAU computer

resents an iteration or a procedure using the Cd bits.

A node is enabled when the operands are ready and the proper context exists. This condition is signaled when all three bits of the control part (C0, C1, and C2) are 1s. The instruction control part detects enabled nodes, using a simulated associative memory, and provides the memory addresses. The addresses in the ICU have a one-to-one correspondence with those in the memory unit. When the memory unit is addressed, it transfers the operation part of an instruction to a first-in-first-out queue that can hold 128 enabled instructions. The top instruction in the FIFO is transferred to an available processing element in the execution unit. The execution unit can support up to 32 processing elements.

A prototype of the LAU architecture with 32 processing elements has been built by the Department of Computer Science, ONERA/CERT, France.

Dynamic Data-Flow Computers

The Manchester Data-Flow Computer. The architecture of the Manchester data-flow computer is shown in Fig. 4–22.

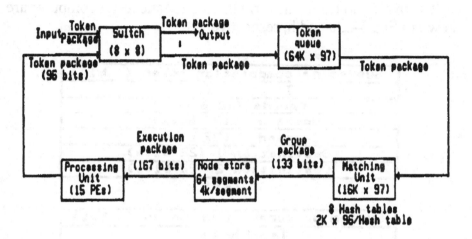

Fig. 4-22. The Manchester data-flow computer

More than one instance of instruction execution is allowed in the Manchester architecture. The race problem, mentioned earlier, is resolved by extending the result packet so that it contains a label field that distinguishes instances of the target instruction.

The designers of the Manchester computer followed the ring topology and used tagged tokens.

Movement of tokens is carried out as follows. A token is transferred from a processing element to a token queue. The queue is used as temporary storage for tokens lying on the arcs of a graph. The matching unit gathers pairs of tokens with the same destination node address and label. Matching is carried out in an associative fashion, so that, when a token arrives at the matching unit, it attempts to match the token with another that has similar matching fields. If no such token is found, the arrived token is kept in the matching unit until a suitable "partner" arrives. A matched pair of tokens that exits the matching unit addresses the node store, to obtain the destination node operation and subsequent destinations of its outputs. Finally, this last combination is transferred to a processing element for execution. The processing unit of the Manchester computer contains 15 processing elements.

The instruction and data formats of the Manchester computer are shown in Fig. 4–23a and b, respectively.

System or computation token (1 bit)
Tag (36 bits)
Opcode (12 bits)
Operand 1 (37 bits)
Operand 2 (37 bits)
Destination 1 (22 bits)
Destination 2 (22 bits)

(a)

System or computation token (1 bit)
Tag (36 bits)
Destination (22 bits)
Value (37 bits)

(b)

Fig. 4-23. Instruction (a) and data token (b) formats
of the Manchester data-flow computer

A prototype system with a single pipeline is in operation at the University of Manchester. The system has been built with transistor-transistor-logic devices.

The Manchester computer uses the language SISAL, which is an extension of the data-flow language VAL. A compiler for SISAL has been developed.

The MIT Dynamic Data-Flow Computer. Only an emulated model, using the Symbolics Corporation's LISP machines at MIT, exists for this proposal, which would allow the dynamic creation of nodes at run time and concurrent execution of several instances of nodes.

The block diagram of the computer is illustrated in Fig. 4–24.

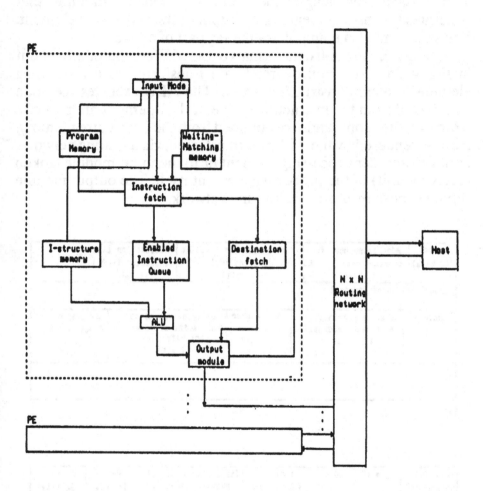

Fig. 4-24. The MIT dynamic data-flow computer

A number of processing elements (the emulated version supports 32) are connected to a switching network in bit-serial fashion. The program memory in each element stores the code associated with nodes. The data memory, labeled I-structure, stores arrays. The waiting-matching store is used to match tokens. The size of the ALU is 32 bits. Each processing element also is equipped with a unit that generates tokens to appear at the output of the processing element. The same unit also manipulates the tag part of a token.

The instruction and data formats of the MIT computer are set out in Fig. 4–25. Code and operands are transferred to a processing element's enabled instruction queue. The ALU executes the code transferred from the instruction queue. If the operands are part of a structure, those operands are obtained from the I-structure memory. Results rendered by the ALU are transferred, via a routing network, either to another processing element or to the input module (token receiving unit) of the processing element itself. The output module supplies those results to the routing network.

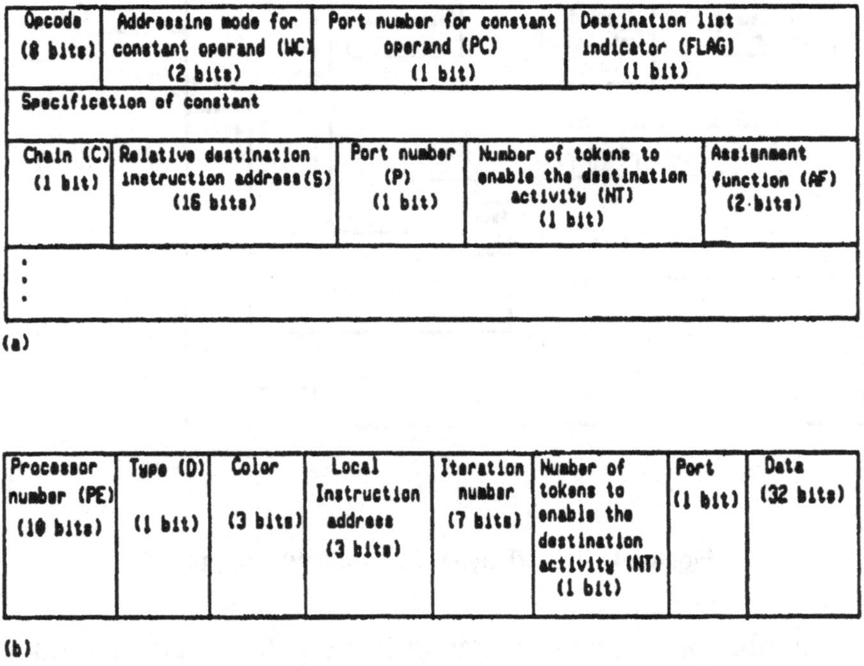

Opcode (8 bits)	Addressing mode for constant operand (WC) (2 bits)	Port number for constant operand (PC) (1 bit)	Destination list indicator (FLAG) (1 bit)		
Specification of constant					
Chain (C) (1 bit)	Relative destination instruction address(S) (16 bits)	Port number (P) (1 bit)	Number of tokens to enable the destination activity (NT) (1 bit)	Assignment function (AF) (2 bits)	
⋮					

(a)

Processor number (PE) (10 bits)	Type (D) (1 bit)	Color (3 bits)	Local Instruction address (3 bits)	Iteration number (7 bits)	Number of tokens to enable the destination activity (NT) (1 bit)	Port (1 bit)	Data (32 bits)

(b)

Fig. 4-25. Instruction (a) and data (b) formats of the MIT dynamic data-flow computer

As do most data-flow computers, the MIT computer depends on a host computer for housekeeping chores, such as downloading of programs.

The DDM1 Computer. This computer, proposed by Davis [8], follows a dynamic architecture without tags. It is a recursively structured machine composed of asynchronous modules and is capable of running tasks concurrently.

Figure 4–26 gives the block diagram of the DDM1 data-flow processor switch element.

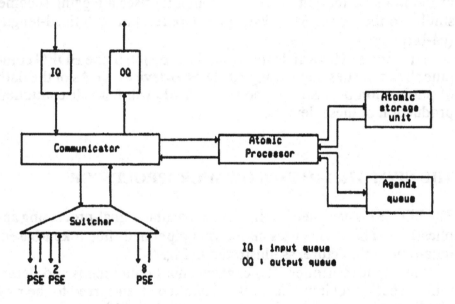

Fig. 4-26. The DDM1 data-flow processor switch element

The DDM1 follows an eight-ary tree structure with a one-of-eight bidirectional switch at each node. The illustration in Fig. 4–26 displays a single processing element, called PSE. Each PSE is assigned a subgraph (task-level node) of a program graph. The high-level graphical functional programming language GPL creates program graphs.

The generation of a program graph is carried out in two stages. In the first stage, GPL statements are translated into data-driven nets (DDN). In the second stage, DDNs are transformed into regular executable graphs (program graphs). These program graphs are transferred to the PSEs in a 4-bit-character serial manner. The communication bus is actually 6 bits, using 2 bits for handshake control (request-acknowledge).

The EDFG Dynamic Data-Flow Computer. Srini also has designed a data-flow computer whose instruction and data formats follow those of the Manchester computer. The computer uses a tagging scheme similar to that of the MIT dynamic computer, but with fixed-length (64-bit) tags.

Srini notes in his article that a bit-slice version of the EDFG computer has been designed, using AMD 2900 devices [9]. As of the date of publication of this book, however, AMD will have discontinued production of these devices.

THE NEC PD7281 DATA-FLOW MICROPROCESSOR

The PD7281 is designed for high-speed, digital, signal-processing applications. The device uses an internal pipelined ring, token-based, data-flow architecture, as illustrated in Fig. 4–27.

The input controller (IC) controls input data tokens and determines whether an input data token should be transferred to the ring pipeline for processing. The output controller (OC) controls output data tokens. The link table (LT) is a 128 x 16-bit buffer that stores instruction parameters. The function table (FT) is another buffer (64 words x 40 bits) that stores instruction parameters. The 512 word x 18-bit data memory (DM) stores constants or temporary data. The queue (Q) is a FIFO buffer (48 words x 60 bits), similar in function to the queues of the other data-flow computers discussed in this chapter. The processing unit (PU) executes arithmetic, logical, and bit operations. The output queue (OQ) (8 words x 32 bits) is similar to the output module of other data-flow computers. The address generator/flow controller (AG/FC) generates addresses for the data memory and controls the flow of tokens. The refresh controller (RC) generates refresh tokens for internal, dynamic random-access memories.

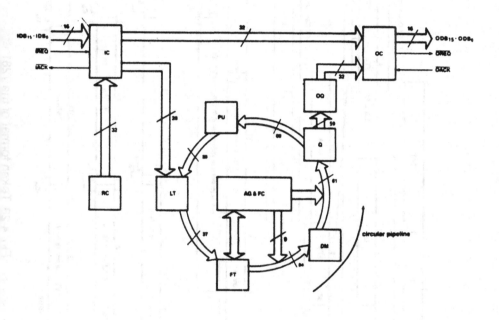

AG/FC – Address generator and flow controller
DM – Data memory
FT – Function table
IC – Input controller
LK – Link table
OC – Output controller

OQ – Output queue
PU – Processing unit
Q – Queue: Data queue (32 words x 60 bits);
Generator queue (16 words x 60 bits)
RC – Refresh controller

Fig. 4-27. Internal architecture of the NEC PD7281

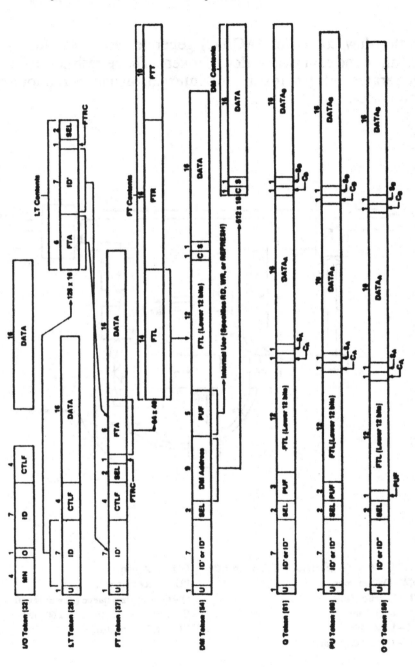

Fig. 4-28 Token format of the 7281

Legend for Fig. 4-28.

C: Control bit for a 16-bit datum
CA: Control bit for a datum from A side
CB: Control bit for a datum from B side
CTLF: Control field
DATA: 16-bit data field
DATA A: 16-bit data from A side
DATA B: 16-bit data from B side
DM Token: Token accessing the data memory
FT Token: Token accessing the function table
FTA: Function table address
FTL: Function table left field
FTR:Function table right field
FTRC: Function table right field control bit
FTT: Function table temporary field

ID: Identifier for an input or output token
ID': Identifier for a token that exits LT for the 1st time
ID": Identifier for a token that exits LT for the 2nd time
I/O Token: Input or output token
LT Token: Token accessing link table
MN: Modulo number
OQ Token: Token accessing the output queue
PU Token: Token accessing the processing unit
PUF: Processing unit flags
Q Token: Token accessing the queue
S: Sign bit for a 16-bit datum
SA: Sign bit for a datum from A side
SB: Sign bit for a datum from B side
SEL: Selection field

The general token format of the 7281 is illustrated in Fig. 4–28. A data token flowing within the ring pipeline must have at least a 7-bit identifier (ID) field and an 18-bit data field. The ID field is used as an address to access the link table memory. When a token accesses the LT memory, the ID field of the token is replaced by a new ID (shown as ID' in Fig. 4–28) previously stored in the LT memory. As a result, every time that a data token accesses LT memory, the ID field of the token is renewed. The data field of a token consists of a control bit, a sign bit, and a 16-bit datum. A token may have up to two data fields, as well as other fields, such as opcode and control.

SUMMARY

This chapter discusses the principal characteristics of data-flow computing. As with other architectures, data flow has its advantages and disadvantages. The disadvantages are of importance when one attempts to design a supercomputer using data-flow principles.

The first consideration arises because parallelism in large-array processing problems is predominantly explicit and, thus, can be handled by the extremely efficient single-instruction-multiple-data stream scheme. Consequently, the ability of a data-flow computer to handle implicit parallelism, which leads to the high control overhead typical of such systems, does not pay.

Second, the pure data-flow scheme is based on the notion that the firing of an operation consumes the tokens that are the carriers of the operands. Consequently, a value can be used as an operand only once. This limitation is counterproductive in all numerical algorithms in which values occur as the operands of a number of operations.

Both of these disadvantages lead to unfavorable speed of program execution.

Manufacturers of VLSI microprocessors have not shown a significant commercial interest in data-flow architectures. Nevertheless, the NEC 7281 appears to have received very favorable comments as a digital signal processing device.

NOTES

[1] John A. Sharp, *Data Flow Computing*, Ellis Horword Limited (Chichester, England: 1988)

[2] Jack B. Dennis, "Data Flow Computers," *Computer* (November 1980)

[3] Vason P. Srini, "An Architectural Comparison of Dataflow Systems," *Computer* (March 1986)

[4] J. B. Dennis and D. P. Misunas, "A Preliminary Architecture for A Basic Dataflow Processor," *Proceedings of 2nd Annual Symposium on Computer Architecture* (New York, NY: May 1975)

[5] K. P. Gostelow and R. E. Thomas, "Performance of a Simulated Dataflow Computer," *I.E.E.E. Transactions on Computers,* C-29, No. 10 (October 1980)

[6] M. Arvind and V. Kathail, "A Multiple Processor That Supports Generalized Procedures," *Proceedings of 8th Annual Symposium on Computer Architecture* (May 1981)

[7] J. Geffin, "A Transputer-based Dataflow Robot Control," *Micro processors,* Microcomputers (May 1990)

[8] A. L. Davis, "The Architecture and System Method of DDM1: A Recursively Structured Data Driven Machine," *Proceedings of 5th Annual Symposium on Computer Architecture* (New York, NY: 1978)

[9] Vason P. Srini, "A Message-based Processor for a Dataflow System," *Proceedings of the International Workshop on High Level Computer Architecture* (Los Angeles, CA: May 1984)

Chapter 5
Case Study: The AM29000

INTRODUCTION

Advanced Micro Devices produces a 32-bit microprocessor, implemented in CMOS technology, which is characterized as a RISC device, although, with more than 100 instructions, the AM29000 fails to fulfill at least one RISC requirement.

The AM29000 has been chosen as a case study in this book because of several interesting features. For example, the manufacturer claims a high number of MIPS (20 MIPS at a 30-MHz operating frequency). This microprocessor is particularly suitable for imbedded applications, such as workstations.

The internal organization of the AM29000 is described first, followed by an architectural, or programming model, description. At the end of this chapter is the simulated execution of a small program, which allows verification of at least the architecture of this microprocessor.

INTERNAL ORGANIZATION

The AM29000 consists of three basic subcircuits: the instruction unit, the execution unit, and the memory-management unit. The entire data flow is shown in Fig. 5-1.

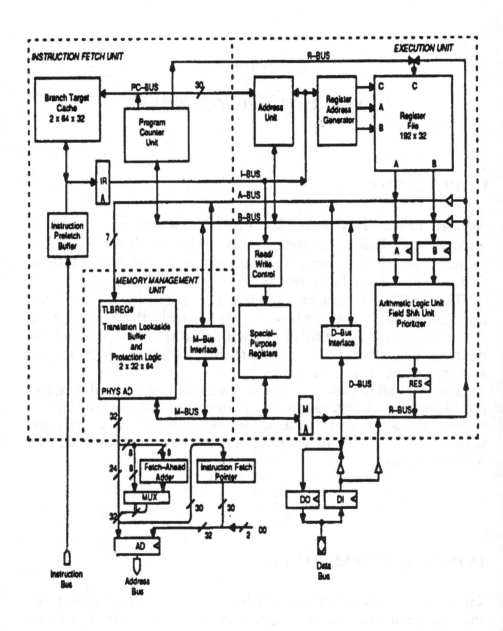

Fig. 5-1. Data flow of the AM29000

Pipeline Structure

A four-stage pipeline is implemented: fetch, decode, execute, and write-back. The pipeline is organized in such a way as to enable the fetch and execution of an instruction in one clock cycle. The manufacturer's data book lists an average of 1.5 clock cycles per instruction. The AM29000 simulator executed a small program at 1.14 cycles (21.87 MIPS @ 25 MHz).

Instructions are fetched by the instruction unit from one of three areas: the instruction prefetch buffer, the branch target cache, or external instruction memory. Instructions are transferred to the decode circuit in the execution unit. The execution unit fetches any operands that the decoded instruction needs; the execution unit also evaluates addresses used in branching, loads, and stores. During execution of an instruction, the memory-management unit performs any required address translation.

The write-back stage is used to store results of an executed instruction. This operation is assisted by the memory-management unit, which performs any required address translation.

Thus, the AM29000 has been designed for maximum performance by optimizing the product of instructions per task, cycles per instruction, and time per cycle — not by minimizing one factor at the expense of others.

Registers

The AM29000 has an abundance of registers, both general-purpose (192) and special-purpose (23). The general-purpose registers are further classified as global (64) and local (128).

Distinction between global and local registers is accomplished via the most-significant bit of a register number. When that bit is 0, a global register is selected; when the most-significant bit is 1, a local register is selected. The bit, however, is not the sole criterion for the selection of a global or local register. The seven least-significant bits of the register number give the global or local register number. For global registers, the absolute-register number is equivalent to the register number. For local registers, the absolute-register number is obtained by adding the local-register number to bits 2 through 8 of the stack pointer and truncating the result to 7 bits.

This addition provides a limited form of base-plus-offset addressing within the local registers. The stack pointer contains the 32-bit base address. This feature assists run-time storage management of variables for dynamically nested procedures. As a result, the AM29000 is designed to minimize the overhead of calling a procedure. The processor allows the functions of passing parameters to a procedure and returning results from a procedure to be performed efficiently. This efficiency is due largely to the definition of local registers. The relative addressing of local registers significantly reduces the overhead of run-time storage management for variables, parameters, returned results, and other quantities required in procedure linkage.

A list of general-purpose registers appears in Fig. 5–2. For the purpose of access restriction, the general-purpose registers are divided into register banks. Except for Bank 0, each bank consists of 16 registers; Bank 0 contains unimplemented Registers 2 through 15. As the list in Fig. 5–2 shows, the register banks are partitioned according to absolute-register numbers. One of the special registers, the register bank protection register, contains 16 protection bits — each of which controls user-mode accesses to a register bank. Bits 0 through 15 of the register bank protection register protect register banks 0 through 15.

Register banking is beneficial, particularly in multitasking applications, when real-time response is more important. With the AM29000 banking scheme, each block is dedicated to a separate process. A task switch can then occur in as few as 17 cycles, or 680 nanoseconds.

All of the general-purpose registers can store variables, addresses, and operating system values. In multitasking applications, the general-purpose registers can be used to hold processor status and variables for as many as eight different tasks. As a result, most instructions can be fetched without the delay of an external access.

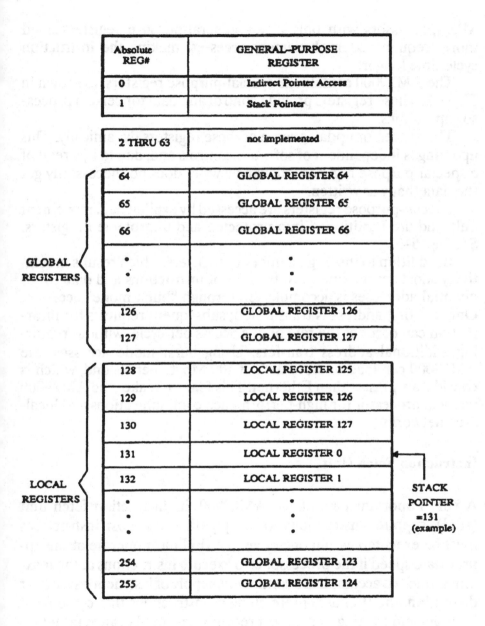

Absolute REG#	GENERAL-PURPOSE REGISTER
0	Indirect Pointer Access
1	Stack Pointer
2 THRU 63	not implemented
64	GLOBAL REGISTER 64
65	GLOBAL REGISTER 65
66	GLOBAL REGISTER 66
. . .	. . .
126	GLOBAL REGISTER 126
127	GLOBAL REGISTER 127
128	LOCAL REGISTER 125
129	LOCAL REGISTER 126
130	LOCAL REGISTER 127
131	LOCAL REGISTER 0
132	LOCAL REGISTER 1
. . .	. . .
254	GLOBAL REGISTER 123
255	GLOBAL REGISTER 124

GLOBAL REGISTERS (64–127)

LOCAL REGISTERS (128–255)

STACK POINTER =131 (example)

Fig. 5-2. List of general-purpose registers

Microprocessors with only a few general-purpose registers need more frequent external memory accesses, making the instruction cycle time longer.

The AM29000 contains 23 special-purpose registers, as shown in Fig. 5–3. These registers provide control and data for certain processor operations.

The processor updates some of these registers dynamically. This updating is independent of software controls and, due to it, a read of a special-purpose register following a write does not necessarily get the data that was written.

Special-purpose registers are accessed by explicit data movement only and are partitioned into protected and unprotected registers. See Fig. 5–3.

In addition to the large number of registers, which results in relatively short access times, fast transfer of instructions and data to sequential addresses is accomplished through "burst mode" accesses. Only the first address is transmitted; subsequent requests for information can occur at the rate of one access per cycle, without requiring additional address transfers. Using burst mode accesses, the AM29000 can load or store data at 100 Mbyte per second, which is considerably faster than Ethernet. This feature makes the AM29000 an ideal processor for high-performance communications and local-area networks.

Instruction Fetch Unit

A very important part of the AM29000, its instruction fetch unit (IFU), supplies instructions to the pipeline. As most instructions must be executed within one cycle, the IFU must operate at the appropriate speed if the processor is to execute instructions at the maximum rate. To accomplish a continuous supply of instructions without disruption, the IFU uses prefetching of instructions that come from memory and caching of the most recently executed branch target instructions.

Prefetching of an instruction takes place at least four cycles

Special Purpose Reg. No.	Protected Registers
0	Vector Area Base Address
1	Old Processor Status
2	Current Processor Status
3	Configuration
4	Channel Address
5	Channel Data
6	Channel Control
7	Register Bank Protect
8	Timer Counter
9	Timer Reload
10	Program Counter 0
11	Program Counter 1
12	Program Counter 2
13	MMU Configuration
14	LRU Recommendation

Special Purpose Reg. No.	Unprotected Registers
128	Indirect Pointer C
129	Indirect Pointer A
130	Indirect Pointer B
131	Q
132	ALU Status
133	Byte Pointer
134	Funnel Shift Count
135	Load/Store Count Remaining

Fig. 5-3. Special-purpose registers

before an instruction is requested for execution. Until a prefetched instruction is needed, it is contained in a four-word instruction prefetch buffer (IPB).

Branch Target Cache

The second area from which instructions are fetched is the branch target cache (BTC). The BTC allows fast access to instructions fetched nonsequentially. A branch instruction may execute in a single cycle, if the branch target is in the BTC.

Operation of the branch target cache lookup is illustrated in Fig. 5–4. A given branch target sequence may be contained in one of two cache blocks, where these blocks are in the same line. The sequence is contained in the line whose number is given by bits 2 through 5 of the address of the first instruction of the sequence. A given branch sequence is in a given cache block only under specific conditions, which need not be described at this point.

Whenever a nonsequential fetch occurs (for a branch instruction, an interrupt, or a trap), the address for the fetch is presented to the branch target cache at the same time that the address is translated by the memory-management unit. If the target instruction for the non-sequential fetch is in the cache, this instruction is presented for decoding during the next cycle. The instruction is always the first in the cache block, and the address of the instruction matches the cache tag. Subsequent instructions in the cache are presented for decoding as required in subsequent cycles. Their addresses, however, do not necessarily match the address tag.

If, on a nonsequential fetch, the target instruction is not found in the branch target cache, the address of the fetch selects a line to be used to store the instruction sequence of the new branch target. The replacement block within the line is selected at random, based on the processor clock. Random replacement has slightly better performance than least-recently-used replacement and has a simpler implementation.

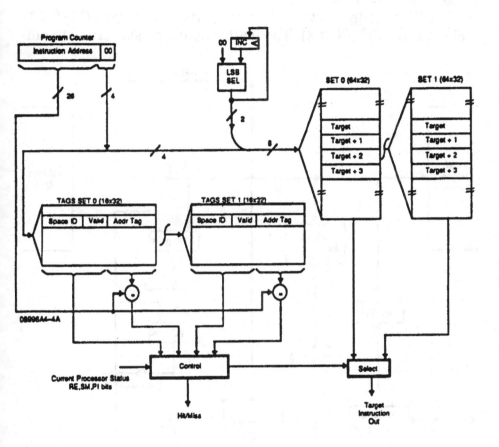

Fig. 5-4. Branch target cache lookup process

Program Counter Unit

The program counter unit of the AM29000, depicted in Fig. 5–5, forms and sequences instruction addresses for the instruction fetch unit. This subunit of the IFU contains the program counter, the program counter multiplexer, the return address latch, and the program counter buffer.

The PC actually is divided into two parts: the master PC (PC L1) and the slave PC (PC L2). The master holds the address of the in-

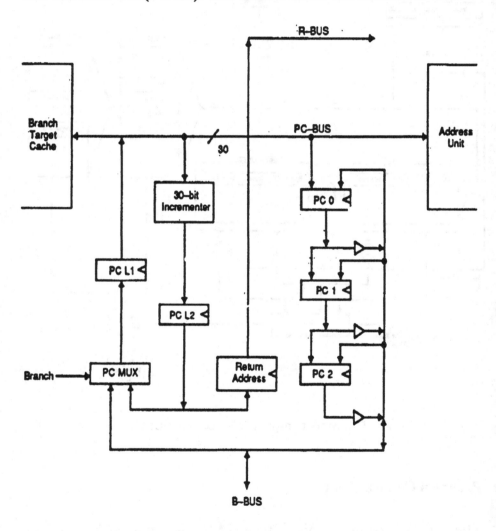

Fig. 5-5. Program counter unit

struction being fetched in the IFU, while the slave holds the next sequential address, which may be fetched by the IFU during the next cycle.

The return address latch holds the address of an instruction following the delayed instruction of a call and transfers that instruction to the register file. This address is the return address of the call.

The PC buffer stores the address of instructions in various stages of execution when an interrupt or trap is taken. Normally, the registers in this buffer — PC0, PC1, and PC2 — are updated from the PC as instructions flow through the processor pipeline.

EXECUTION UNIT

The execution unit of the AM29000 consists of the register file, the address unit, and the arithmetic-logic unit.

Register File

The registers have been discussed in detail in an earlier part of this chapter.

Address Unit

The address unit, shown in Fig. 5–6, computes addresses for branch target instructions and load-multiple and store-multiple sequences. This unit also assembles data for immediate instructions and creates addresses for restarting terminated instruction prefetch streams.

The address unit consists of a 30-bit adder, the decode PC register, the ADRF (address fetch) latch, and logic for formatting the data for immediate instructions and for generating the constants 1 and 0. The decode PC register holds the address of the instruction in the decode stage of the pipeline.

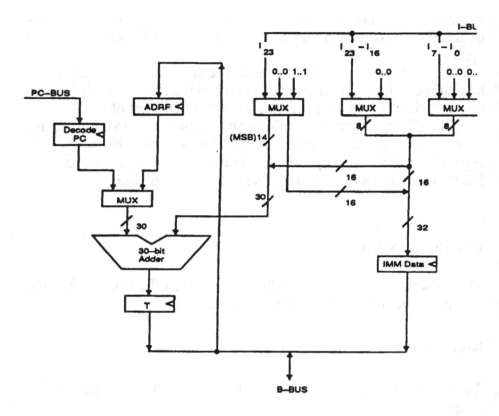

Fig. 5-6. The address unit

Arithmetic-Logic Unit

The ALU of the AM29000 performs the four basic (32-bit) arithmetic operations, including those that involve carry. The ALU also performs logic operations (all 32 bit), such as AND, OR, NAND, NOR, A AND-NOT B, XOR, and XNOR, and evaluates relational expressions with the operators equal, not-equal, less-than, less-than-or-equal, greater-than, and greater-than-or-equal. The relational operators may be applied to either signed or unsigned operands.

MEMORY-MANAGEMENT UNIT

A key feature of the integral memory-management unit of the AM29000 includes a 64-entry, two-way, set-associative translation look-aside buffer (t.l.b), which performs the virtual-to-physical address translation. So as to be more efficient, this operation is pipelined to run in parallel with other processor operations.

Other features of the memory-management unit include 4 gigabytes of virtual memory per process for up to 256 processes; pipelined address translation to reduce latency; software t.l.b. reload, allowing user-defined, memory-management architecture for maximum flexibility; and least-recently-used hardware to assist reload and memory protection. Software t.l.b. reload allows system designers to choose a memory-management scheme best matched to the particular environment: for example, page selection of 1, 2, 4, or 8 Kbytes. The t.l.b. reload performance is enhanced by least-recently-used hardware, as well as a low trap overhead.

DEVELOPMENT TOOLS

One of the nice features of the AM29000 family of microprocessors is the abundance of development tools, both hardware and software. A brief description of some of these features follows.

Hardware

The PCEB29K IBM PC board can be inserted into an IBM PC/XT/AT and compatible computers. The PCEB29K allows the user to evaluate and apply the processing power of the AM29000 processor to a variety of applications. In addition to the AM29000 processor and control logic, the board is equipped with a hefty 512 Kbytes of DRAM.

The PCEB29K is controlled by a software monitor that offers

many useful functions for the development of applications programs, such as the display or modification of memory and registers, in-line assembly or disassembly of a program, file system support, and C run-time support. The last function allows programs written for the PCEB29K board to use all functions in the ANSI C library except system( ).

An example of a memory dump, using the PCEB29K's "ebmon" monitor is shown in Fig. 5–7. In addition to the contents of global and local registers, the ALU and flag statuses also are shown.

```
# DW LR0
LR000    00000000  00000000  00000000  00000000  ..............
LR004    00000000  00000000  00000000  00000000  ..............
LR008    00000000  00000000  00000000  00000000  ..............
LR012    00000000  00000000  00000000  00000000  ..............
LR016    00000000  00000000  00000000  00000000  ..............
LR020    00000000  00000000  00000000  00000000  ..............
LR024    00000000  00000000  00000000  00000000  ..............
LR028    00000000  00000000  00000000  00000000  ..............
```

Fig. 5-7. Memory dump using the PCEB29K's software monitor

```
# y : pi -100
# gi
Console controlled by Am29000 — enter Ctrl-A to return to monitor.
        The value of pi to 100 decimal places

        3.14159265358979323846264338327950288419716939937510
          58209749445923078164062862089986280348253421170681

#0000a9d0I    JMPTI      GR121,LR0
#
```

Fig. 5-8. Calculation of pi to 100 decimal places

Another nice feature of the ebmon monitor allows programs that require arguments to be passed to them when they are started to be invoked by placing the arguments after the file name when loading the file to memory. The program example "pi -100," shown after the "y :" load from memory command in Fig. 5–8, instructs the PCEB29K to calculate the value of pi to 100 decimal places.

The ADAPT29K advanced development and prototyping tool is another hardware item that Advanced Micro Devices offers for software and hardware development around the AM29000.

The ADAPT29K has a software monitor similar to that of the PCEB29K (same commands). Unlike the PCEB29K, however, the ADAPT29K can be used as a stand-alone or remote system, as shown in Fig. 5–9.

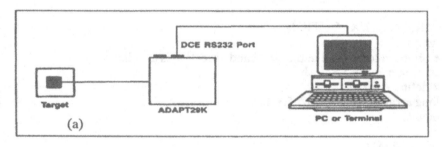

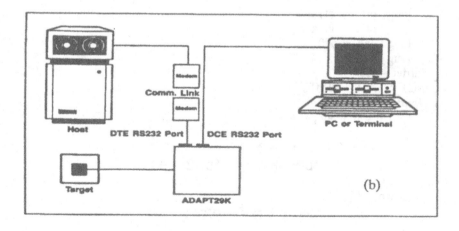

Fig. 5-9. ADAPT29K development tool used as
(a) a stand-alone unit or (b) a remote unit

Software

Advanced Micro Devices offers a wide selection of software tools, including the ASM29K cross assembler\linker, the HighC29K ANSI C compiler, and the XRAY29K source-level debugger. Most may be used under DOS or UNIX.

Another useful tool is the AM29000 architecture simulator, which provides a thorough picture of the behavior of the AM29000 during the execution of a program. An example of the simulator's work is shown in Fig. 5 – 10.

SIMULATED EXECUTION
Program
The program to be used in the simulated execution is as follows:

```
#include <MIO>    .h
#define AMD 1
long array1[ 500 ], array2[ 500 ] ;
main()
{
#ifdef AMD
#include "timing.h"
#endif
   long *ptr1 = array1 ;
   long *ptr2 = array2 ;
   long i, len = 500 ;
   long j ;
#ifdef AMD
GET_START_TIME
#endif
   for ( j = 0; j 50; j + + )
   {
      for ( i = 0; i len; i + + )
                *ptr1 + +  =  *ptr2 + + ;
      i = len ;
      while ( i– )
                * –ptr1 = * –ptr2 ;
   }
#ifdef AMD
GET_END_TIME
CALC_TIME
```

```
    PRINT_TIME
    #endif
    exit(0);
    }
Timing.h
    /*
    * AMD cycle timer header file.
    */
    unsigned long _start_time;
    unsigned long _end_time;
    unsigned long -ovrhd;
    unsigned long _total time;
    #define GET_START_TIME  _start_time = _cycles(); \
                            _end_time = _cycles(); \
                            _ovrhd = _end_time - _start_time; \
                            _start_time = _cycles();
    #define GET_END_TIME    _end_time = _cycles();
    #define CALC_TIME       _total_time = _end_time - _start_time - _ovrhd;
    #define PRINT_TIME printf"Time to execute this routine : \0\0\0"); \
                       print("%u cycles\n\0\0\0", _total_time);
Test.lst
    Loading AM29000 Memory from file: a.out.
    Loading section '.text' at address 00008000 [3ec0 bytes of type text]
    Loading section '.lit' at address 0000c000 [13c bytes of type data or lit]
    Loading section '.data' at address 0000e000 [520 bytes of type data or lit]
    Loading section '.data1' at address 00010000 [34 bytes of type data or lit]
    Loading section '.bss' at address 00012000 [11fc bytes of type bss]
    Loading ROM from file: /usr/local/hc_r2.0.0/29k/lib/osboot.
    Loading section '.text' at address 00000000 [525cbytes of type ROM text]
    Loading section '.data' at address 00005260 [2c4 bytes of type data or lit]
    Loading section '.bss' at address 00005528 [24 bytes of type bss]
    Heap allocated at address 00013200 [8000 bytes]
    Entry at Address: 00008004
    Simulation Start Time: Thur.Apr.5 19:27:38 1990
    Time to execute this routine: 400559 cycles
    Simulation complete. — successful termination
    ------------------------------------------------------------------
    Simulation Results of AM29000 "Rev-C"
    Simulation Completion Time: Tue Nov 21 19:53:16 1989


    Environment of "a.out" simulation:

        CPU Clock Frequency: 25.000 Mhz
```

Instruction Memory:
40 ns for a Simple access. (0 Wait States)
40 ns for 1st Burst access & 40 ns during. (Auto-Pipelining)
(0 ns To Decode an Address)

Instruction ROM Memory:
40 ns for a Simple access. (0 Wait States)
No Burst accesses are allowed and no Pipelined accesses are allowed.
(0 ns To Decode an Address)

Data Memory:
40 ns for a Simple access. (0 Wait States)
40 ns for 1st Burst access & 40 ns during. (Auto-Pipelining)
(0 ns To Decode an Address)

Statistics of a.out: simulation (V6.0-8):

User Mode: 408350 cycles (0.01633400 seconds)
Supervisor Mode: 1654 cycles (0.00006616 seconds)
Total: 410004 cycles (0.01640016 seconds)
Instructions Executed: 358632

Simulation speed: 21.87 MIPS (1.14 cycles per instruction)

----------Pipeline----------
12.53% idle pipeline:
0.20% Instruction Fetch Wait
12.24% Data Transaction Wait
0.00% Page Boundary Crossing Fetch Wait
0.00% Unfilled Cache Fetch Wait
0.01% Load/Store Multiple Executing
0.06% Load/Load Transaction Wait
0.02% Pipeline Latency

----------Branch Target Cache----------
Branch cache access: 204416
Branch cache hits: 202909
Branch cache hit ratio: 99.26%

----------Translation Look-aside Buffer----------
TLB access: 0
TLB hits: 0
TLB hit ratio: 0.00%

```
----------Bus Utilization----------
Inst Bus Utilization: 62.82%
    57578 Instruction Fetches

Data Bus Utilization: 24.72%
    50681 Loads
    50675 Stores

----------Instruction Mix----------
    0.04% Calls
    14.40% Jumps
    14.13% Loads
    14.13% Stores
    0.10% No-ops

----------Register File Spilling/Filling----------
    0 Spills
    0 Fills
```

Fig. 5-10. Program used for the simulation (a) and
actual output of the simulator (b)

SUMMARY

The AM29000 displays an undoubted high performance and is suitable for many applications where real-time or extremely fast data processing is required. Such applications may include embedded control, engineering and scientific workstations, and robot control.

In ISDN networks, the AM29000 also provides excellent performance. Applications likely to benefit especially from the AM29000 include graphics, robotics, simulation, and array processing.

Chapter 6
Case Study: The Inmos Transputer

INTRODUCTION

Transputers, built by the British company INMOS, are indeed revolutionary microprocessors. Evaluation of the internal architecture and performance of a transputer reveals that this type of device is several years ahead of its competitors.

A transputer has a von Neumann architecture, but, unlike conventional microprocessors, a transputer may be configured into networks and arrays, in which each transputer executes its own processes — sequences of instructions — using its own local memory. Thus, concurrency may be achieved. A system has as many buses as it has transputers, and the resultant bus throughput is a product of the number of transputers in the system.

A transputer may be programmed in Parallel C, Parallel Fortran, Parallel Pascal, and other high-level languages. However, the programming language OCCAM2 has been designed specifically to exploit the concurrency feature of the transputer, since Occam is designed to allow a complex application to be stated as a collection of processes that operate concurrently while communicating through channels.

HARDWARE DESCRIPTION OF TRANSPUTER

Inmos produces a variety of transputers, ranging in size between 16 and 32 bits. Among the most popular are the T414, which has 2 kilobytes of on-chip memory, and the T800.

The IMS T800 transputer is a 32-bit CMOS microprocessor, equipped with an on-chip, 64-bit, floating-point coprocessor and graphics support. The T800 has 4 kilobytes of on-chip RAM for high-speed processing, a configurable memory interface, and four standard serial input-output communication links. Figure 6–1 shows the block diagram of the T800.

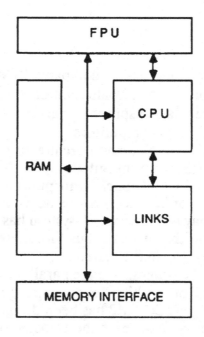

Fig. 6-1. Block diagram of the IMS T800

A transputer executes processes, or sequences of instructions. A process starts, carries out a number of actions, and then either stops without completing the execution or terminates on complete execution of the process. At any time, a process may be active (executing or waiting on a list to be executed) or inactive (ready to input, ready to output, or waiting a specified time).

A microcoded scheduler enables any number of concurrent processes, by allocating a portion of the processor's time to each process in turn. Processes, thus, share the processor's time, and the need for a software kernel is removed.

The scheduler operates to ensure that inactive processes do not consume time. Active processes waiting to be executed are held in two linked lists of process workspaces, one of high-priority processes and one of low-priority processes. Each list is implemented using two registers, one of which points to the first process in the list while the other points to the last. Observe, in Fig. 6–2, that process S is executing and processes P, Q, and R are active, awaiting execution. Only the low-priority process queue registers are shown in Fig. 6–2. The high-priority process registers perform in a similar manner.

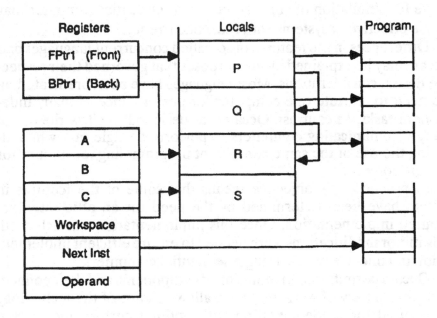

Fig. 6-2. Linked process list

Each process runs until it has completed its action, but, while waiting for communication from another process or another transputer or due to a time delay, the process is descheduled. For several processes to operate in parallel, a low-priority process is permitted to run only for a maximum of two time slices before it is necessarily descheduled at the next available descheduling point. Descheduling points are certain instructions such as "input message" and "output byte."

LANGUAGE

Many languages have been designed to simulate concurrency, for, until recently, concurrency was not economically feasible. Inherent in any simulation is the question of accuracy. Furthermore, a language for simulation of concurrency on a sequential computer may not be effective in systems with real concurrency.

Differences in the features of so-called concurrent languages and Occam may be explained by the purposes that governed their respective design considerations. Most languages have been predicated on the need to allocate one computer for performance of many independent tasks. In contrast, Occam was designed to allow the use of many communicating computers to perform a single task while allowing the use of the same concurrent programming techniques for a single computer.

In practice, this objective means that some of the features in Occam have been determined by the need for an efficiently distributed implementation. Once this implementation was achieved, only minor modifications were needed to ensure efficient implementation of concurrency on a single sequential computer.

Occam permits implementation of components and their connections in a variety of ways and, thus, allows choice of the technology best suited for implementation with optimal performance at the lowest cost.

Although Occam is a relatively small language, it supports a wide variety of programming techniques. Facially, Occam2 has similarities to Pascal, such as procedures. Unlike Pascal, however, Occam2 is not portable.

Occam addresses the bottlenecking problem of a von Neumann-type, bus-oriented architecture by allowing larger systems to be expressed in terms of localized processing and communication. The effective use of concurrency requires new algorithms designed to exploit this hierarchical decomposition.

Primary objectives of Occam are, therefore, its direct implementation by a network of processing elements and direct expression of concurrent algorithms. In many respects, Occam acts as an assembler with a one-to-one relationship between Occam processes and processing elements and between Occam channels and links between processing elements.

Occam can express locality of processing by each process having local variables. Thus, Occam can express locality of communication in that each channel connects only two processes.

Programming is greatly simplified with synchronized, zero-buffered communication, which obviates the need for message buffers and queues and prevents accidental data loss due to programming errors. Scheduling and timing may be sensitive issues in an unsynchronized scheme.

A brief description of Occam follows. In the examples, note that the structure of the program is shown through indentation by exactly two spaces. Semicolons are unnecessary. Pictorial representations should correspond to program text directly, to aid in the design of a concurrent algorithm that is efficient to implement.

Primitive Processes and Constructs

Programs in Occam consist of three primitive processes, which, in combination, form other processes, called constructs. The primitive processes are:

v :e	assign expression e to variable v
c ! e	output expression e to channel c
c ? v	input variable v from channel c.

The constructs, which may themselves be part of other constructs, are:

ALT   alternative
IF   conditional
PAR   parallel
SEQ   sequence

The transputer has simple hardware and only a small number of microcoded instructions. Consequently, implementation of Occam is straightforward, with instructions that define "kernel" primitives for other implementations of Occam. The resultant efficiency is about 1 microsecond per component of PAR and 1.5 microsecond per process communication.

Note also that process interactions in Occam are direct representations of hardware mechanisms.

The constructs will be described in greater detail later in this chapter. It should be noted here, however, that Occam affords the flexibility of both concurrent and sequential behavior. Thus, a conventional sequential program may be expressed through conditional and sequential constructs that combine assignments and variables.

A conventional iterative is possible with a while loop. As in other modern programming languages, there is an absence of explicit transfers of control. For Occam, this absence obviates the need to prohibit or define a transfer out of a parallel component or procedure.

Through alternative and parallel constructs, concurrent programs are formed through the combination of channels, inputs, and outputs.

Occam procedures are defined and used in accordance with ALGOL-type rules on scope for channel, variable, and value parameters. The body of a procedure may be any parallel or sequential construct.

Figure 6–3 depicts a simple Occam program for a buffer process.

```
WHILE TRUE
    VAR ch:
        SEQ                     in----- >        ch        ---- >
            in ? ch
            out ! ch
```

Fig. 6-3. Occam program of buffer process

The buffer in Fig. 6–3 is an endless loop, in which the variable "ch," declared by "VAR ch," is set to a value from the channel "in" and then is outputted to the channel "out."

Compiler

Figure 6–4 shows the structure of an Occam compiler. Sections of programs "fold" away, so that only the comment is visible.

```
CHAN lexed.program:
CHAN parsed.program:
CHAN scoped.program:
PAR
    -- lexer
CHAN name.text:
CHAN name.code:
PAR
    -- scanner
    -- nametable
    -- parser
CHAN parsed.lines:
PAR
    -- line parser
    -- construct parser
    -- scoper
    -- generator
CHAN generated.constructs:
CHAN generated.program:
PAR
    -- construct generator
    -- line generator
    -- space allocator
```

Fig. 6-4. Compiler

Only messages from the lexical analyzer modify data in the nametable process. Figure 6–5 shows initialization.

```
--nametable
SEQ
    --initialize
    WHILE going
        -- input text of name
        -- look up name
        -- output corresponding code
    --terminate
```

Fig. 6-5. Initialization of nametable

The compiler functions as a multiple-pass compiler, although facially it seems to be a single-pass compiler. Each process performs a simple transformation on the data that flows through the process. Decomposition of the compiler in this manner makes each component process relatively easy to write, specify, and test. Consequently the component processes may be written concurrently.

The compiler must monitor a number of restrictions applicable to the components of a parallel construct. The components may communicate only through channels that afford one-way communication. Thus, one component exclusively inputs to the channel, while another component solely outputs from the channel. Components may not share access to variables.

Hierarchical Decomposition

Occam allows a process to be separated into concurrent component processes, through the use of named communication channels. This allows the use of Occam for large applications, because the parallel construct, and named channels, would allow the application to be decomposed into a hierarchy of communicating processes. This is a capability unavailable in languages that use process, or entry, names for communication.

When a channel exists between processes, those processes do not need to know anything about the internal details, which may, in fact, change during execution of a program.

Channel protocol must be specified, in order to specify the behavior of a process. Consideration must be given to the mode of channel protocol that suits not only the individual program but, indeed, the particular channel that the protocol is to serve. Thus, for messages between processes in a linear pipeline, the Bachus-Naur form may be appropriate. Figure 6–6 demonstrates, however, that a streamlined Occam program allows easier examination of complex interactions between processes, without reference to data values.

```
SEQ
    request ?
WHILE TRUE
PAR
    reply !
    request ?
```

```
WHILE TRUE            SEQ                 SEQ
    SEQ                   request !           request !
        request!          WHILE TRUE          WHILE TRUE
        reply ?           SEQ                 PAR
                             request             request !
                             reply !             reply ?
```

Fig. 6-6. Easier examination of complex interactions

Alternative Construct

In an Occam program, a process sometimes will need input from one or more concurrent processes. In some instances, this requirement may be met efficiently enough through a channel test, which is true only if ready. Since, however, the process must poll its inputs "busily," a channel test will not always be efficient. Therefore, Occam has an alternative construct, which may be implemented either with a channel test or with a "nonbusy" scheme.

A fuller description of this construct may be obtained by reference to [1]. It is sufficient for our purposes to note merely that the alternative construct of Occam is similar to that of CSP [2]. Thus, each component begins with a guard, which is an input coupled, sometimes, with a Boolean expression.

In Occam, a guard does not fail automatically on termination of a process that is connected to the guard through the channel. Any convenience of this programming feature is outweighed by the complication in protocol for channel communication, since additional types of messages would be needed. Moreover, explicit expression of termination can make programs clearer.

Parallel Construct

As Fig. 6–7 expresses formally, a parallel construct dictates that the components be "executed together." Consequently, the order of component primitive processes is not structured.

```
PAR                 =           SEQ
   SEQ                             x: = e
      x: = e                    PAR
      P                            P
   Q                             Q
```

Fig. 6-7. PARallel and SEQuential constructs

As noted, synchronized communication demands that a process wait for another. Nonetheless, it is easy to write a process that continues while communicating. See Fig. 6–8.

```
PAR
   c ! x
   P
```

Fig. 6-8. Process continues while communicating

Arrays

Occam has a unique form for representation of arrays, which is described fully in [3]. This form is not related to concurrency.

Several considerations should dictate the relationship between an array declaration and a loop that performs an operation for each element of the array. First, the relationship should be uncomplicated. Second, the number of elements in the array or the number of iterations in the loop should be easily visible. Figure 6–9 gives alternative representations. It is apparent that the second alternative better fulfills the requirements of simplicity and visibility. Further, an "empty" loop corresponds to count = 0, rather than limit¡base, so that an unsatisfactory loop FOR i IN [0 TO -1] is unnecessary. All arrays start from 0, so implementation is further simplified.

alternative 1: ARRAY a [base TO limit]
FOR i IN [base TO limit]
alternative 2: ARRAY a [base FOR count]
FOR i IN [base FOR count]

Fig. 6-9. Alternatives to relationship between array and loop

The rules that govern channels and variables have been adjusted for arrays of channels and variables. If an assignment changes a component of an array, the array may not be used in any other component. Multiple components of a parallel may not use channels from a single array, through variable subscripts. A component of a parallel that uses an array for input and output may not use variable channels to choose channels from the array. Variable subscript denotes a subscript that the compiler cannot evaluate.

Earlier versions of Occam had only unidimensional arrays, but now multidimensional arrays also are provided.

Replicator

A "for" loop in Occam is generalized and has simplified semantics.

Figure 6–10 sets out a formula for definition of a replicator in Occam. A replicator may be used with any of the constructs, which is denoted by X in Fig. 6–10. B and c are expressions. N is a name, for the control variable, which is defined implicitly and, thus, is not changed by assignments within P.

```
X n = b FOR c              = X
      P(n)                      P(b)
                                P(b+1)
                                ...
                                P(b+c-1)
```

Fig. 6-10. Replicator in Occam

Time

In Occam, time corresponds to a conventional clock, as it cycles through integer values. A value sufficiently large to break the cycle is theoretically possible, but not justifiable, because the use of multiple-length arithmetic would be needed for the clock.

So that a program does not wait busily for a particular time, a process needs to be able to read the clock at any time. Therefore, a timer is declared, in the same manner that channels and variables are. Localized timers exist.

To read time, a special input "time ? v" is used. The input "time ? AFTER t" waits for time t.

In Occam, a process cannot implement a timer, although the requisite timer output "timer ! PLUS n", which would advance the timer by n ticks, is simple and would facilitate construction of timers with different rates and writing of a process for simulation of time.

Types and Data Structures

Various versions of Occam exist. The first version had untyped variables but addressing operations, for the compiler would be unable to check variables not shared by concurrent processes.

Occam now has Boolean, integer, and byte data types. Any type may be used so long as its input and output values can be as signed in accordance with the following rule:

```
PAR
    c ! x   =   y : = x
    c ? y
```

Type conversions are, therefore, not recommended.

Communication and assignment operate on variables of any type and, thus, allow arrays to be communicated and assigned.

Compile-Time Allocation

Allocation of processors and memory at compile time is clearly advantageous in terms of run-time efficiency, but the compiler needs to be able to determine the amount of space demanded for each component of a parallel construct. Consequently, the number of components in an array and the number of concurrent processes that a parallel replicator will create must be known. With these restrictions, the run-time overhead of a parallel construct is very small. Occam, however, does not impose these restrictions inherently.

Figure 6–11 depicts alternative methods for decription of a tree of processors. The first alternative uses recursive Occam, while the second alternative avoids recursiveness. The latter, however, requires the depth of the tree to be known at compile time, as would normally be the case for a program to be executed on a fixed-size processor array.

```
PROC tree (VALUE n, CHAN down, CHAN up)
    IF
        no = 0
            leaf ( down, up )
        n > 0
            CHAN left.down, left.up
            CHAN right.down, right.up
        PAR
            tree (n-1, left.down, left.up)
            tree (n-1, right.down, right.up)
            node ( down, up, left.down, left.up, right.down, right.up )
DEF p = TABLE [1, 2, 4, 8, 16, 32, 64, 128] :
--depth of tree = n
CHAN down [n*(n-1)] :
CHAN up [n*(n-1)] :


PAR
    PAR i - [0 FOR n-1]
        PAR j = [0 FOR p[i]]
            branch ( down [p[i] + j], up [p[i] + j], down
                [p[i+1] = (j*2)], up [p[i+1] + (j*2)], down
                [p[i+1] + (j*2) + 1], up [p[i+1] + (j*2) + 1] )
    PAR i = [0 FOR p[n]]
        leaf ( down [p[n] + i], up [p[n] + i] )
```

Fig. 6-11. Alternative methods for description of tree of processors

To ensure a correctness-preserving transformation between the programs in Fig. 6–11, a preprocessor could be used.

Program Development

Occam greatly reduces a common problem in design of a multiprocessor system, in which the most effective configuration is not immediately clear and, therefore, to the extent possible, design and programming should be completed before construction of hardware begins. Since the concurrency programming techniques in Occam are equally applicable to single computers and networks of computers, a program may be compiled and executed on one computer during program development, even if ultimately the program is intended for a network.

Furthermore, the constructs PAR and ALT result in a clear indication of "logical behavior," with respect to those aspects of the programs that real-time effects do not govern. Mapping of processes and the speed of processing and communication do not alter logical behavior. With respect to PAR, implementation may execute arbitrarily any of the several components that may be ready, and not waiting to communicate. For ALT, arbitrary implementation again is available, without regard to the "earliest."

Configuration

Annotation of ALT and PAR provides the configuration that a program needs to satisfy real-time constraints.

Prioritization of components may be used with either construct, although in practice, prioritization is used infrequently. Its effect is demonstrated in Fig. 6–12. Compare Fig. 6–12 with the program in Fig. 6–5.

```
WHILE going
    PRI ALT
        stop ? ANY
            going : = FALSE
        in ? ch
        out ! ch
```

Fig. 6-12.

Figure 6–13 demonstrates how a prioritized ALT allows either a prioritized or "fair" multiplexer.

```
WHILE TRUE -- prioritized
  PRI ALT i = 0 FOR 10
    in [i] ? ch
    out ! ch
WHILE TRUE -- fair
  PRI ALT i = 0 FOR 10
    in [(i + last) REM 10] ? ch
    SEQ
      out ! ch
      last : = (i + 1) REM 10
```

Fig. 6-13. Prioritized ALT

As noted, prioritization is not used frequently because, eventually, processes that are consuming all of the processing resources must stop and wait for other processes. If not, the other processes are redundant and should not be in the program.

Scheduling becomes important if, for example, multiple users of the system may impose disjointed demands.

Programs

The most salient feature of Occam is the choice that it affords to a programmer, who may use a concurrent or sequential algorithm. Most programs consist of both, with a concurrent algorithm that describes a network of transputers and sequential algorithms that the transputers execute.

Writing the concurrent algorithm first has been suggested as best [4], because only that algorithm affords freedom in implementation. As an example, transputers, in the number needed for performance although not more than 10, may be connected to form a pipeline. A sequential program is not so easily adaptable.

Again refer to Fig. 6–11 and compare Fig. 6–14, in which a concurrent searching algorithm is implemented. The leaf processors hold the data to be searched. The node processors disperse the data and collect the replies.

```
PROC leaf (CHAN down, up) =
  VAR data, enq:
  SEQ
    ... -- load data
    WHILE TRUE
      SEQ
        down ? enq
        up ! (enq = data)
PROC node (CHAN down, up, CHAN left.down, left.up,
            CHAN right.down, right.up) =
WHILE TRUE
  VAR enq, left.found, right.found :
  SEQ
    down ? enq
    PAR
      left.down ! enq
      right.down ! enq
    PAR
      left.up ? left.found
      right.up ? right.found
    up ! left.found OR right.found
```

Fig. 6-14.

A conventional sequential searching algorithm that operates on the array of data avoids the waste that results if each leaf stored only one item of data, although, in fact, each leaf could execute the concurrent algorithm, through a tree of processes. Figure 6-15 provides the modified program.

```
PROC leaf (CHAN down, up) =
  VAR enq, data [length], found
  SEQ
    ... -- initialize data
    WHILE TRUE
      SEQ
        found : = FALSE
        down ? enq
        SEQ i = [0 FOR length]
          found : = (data [i] = enq ) OR found
        up ! found :
```

Fig. 6-15.

The number of items to be held in each leaf should be chosen so that the time for dispersal of the inquiry and collection of the response is short in comparison with the time for a search of each leaf. Assume that the time for communication is 5 microseconds. Then, in a tree with a depth of seven (128 leaves), communication requires only about 70 microseconds, or 10% of the time needed to search 1000 items.

Many concurrent algorithms need merely PAR and a communication channel for concurrency. Among these algorithms is the "systolic" array, which Occam allows to be written in two ways. Refer to Fig. 6–16, which describes a conventional synchronous array processor. Data is taken from the master register and computed in parallel, with the result left in the slave register. Synchronization is global — i.e., operations start and terminate together during each iteration as the data moves along the pipeline. The first output will be garbage, as initialization has been omitted. As the size of the array increases, the speed of the program reduces.

```
VAR master [ n ]:
VAR slave [ n ]:
WHILE TRUE
  SEQ
    PAR i = 0 FOR n
      compute (master [ i ] , slave [ i ])
    PAR
      input ? master [ 0 ]
      PAR i = 0 FOR n-1
        master [ i + 1 ] : = slave [ i ]
      output ! slave [ n ]
```

Fig. 6-16. Description of a synchronous array processor

Figure 6–17 shows another program, in which "c[0]" and "c[n + 1]" are the input and output channels, respectively. Although the operations are performed together, initialization is unnecessary, as no output results until the first input has passed through the pipeline. The pipeline synchronizes itself, as needed to communicate data.

```
CHAN c [ n + 1 ] :
PAR i = 0 FOR n
    WHILE TRUE
        VAR d:
        VAR r:
        SEQ
            c [ n ] ? d
            compute ( d,r)
            c [ n + 1 ] ! r
```

Fig. 6-17.

Output Guards

Occam does not include output guards, although, as described later, they may be generated.

Figure 6–18 contains two programs for a buffer process – one that uses output guards and one that uses Occam without output guards. It is immediately evident that the use of output guards allows a simpler program, allowing it to be written in a more natural manner. Consequently, there have been attempts to include output guards in Occam.

Distributed implementation is the primary stumbling block. Examination of the program in Fig. 6–18 demonstrates the problem that arises if, for example, two or more processors enter their alternative construct simultaneously. This problem may be handled by the assignment of a unique number to each processor in a system but with commensurate complication of the protocol for communication.

Nonetheless, Occam may be used to write a communication kernel that gives a version of Occam with output guards.

```
WHILE TRUE
   ALT
      count <0 & output ! buff [outpointer]
         SEQ
            outpointer: = (outpointer + 1) REM max
            count : = count -1
      count < max & input ? buff [inpointer]
         SEQ
            inpointer : = (inpointer + 1) REM max
            count : = count + 1
PAR
   WHILE TRUE
      ALT
         count >0 & req ? ANY
            SEQ
               reply ! buff [outpointer]
               outpointer : = (outpointer + 1) REM max
               count : = count - 1
         count < max & input ? buff [inpointer]
            SEQ
               inpointer : = (inpointer + 1) REM max
               count : = count + 1
   WHILE TRUE
      SEQ
         req ! ANY
         reply ? ch
         output ! ch
```

Fig. 6-18. Programs for buffer process

SUMMARY

A transputer, coupled with a specially designed language such as Occam, affords a degree of concurrency unattainable even a few short years ago. Furthermore, careful consideration in the design of hardware and software makes use of the transputer relatively simple.

NOTES

[1] A. W. Roscoe and C. A. R. Hoare, *The Laws of Occam Program ming*, Programming Research Group, Oxford University (1986)

[2] G. N. Buckley and A. Silberschatz, "An Effective Implementation for the Generalized Input-Output Construct of CSP," *ACM Transactions on Programming Languages and Systems,* 5 (April 1983) p. 224.

[3] C. A. R. Hoare, "Communicating Sequential Processes," *Communications of the ACM,* 2, No. 1 8 (August 1978), p. 666

[4] A. W. Roscoe and C. A. R. Hoare, *The Laws of Occam Program ming,* Programming Research Group, Oxford University (1986)

Chapter 7

Microprocessors for Signal and Image Processing

INTRODUCTION

Digital signal microprocessors appeared in the early 1980s. These devices are able to perform extremely fast multiplications and additions. This ability is particularly beneficial for tasks that require repetitive calculations — e.g., filtering, speech and handwriting recognition, and image processing and enhancement.

There are essentially two types of digital signal processors — i.e., low- to medium-performance devices and high-performance devices dedicated to a specific application area.

TEXAS INSTRUMENTS' TMS320 FAMILY

Texas Instruments has been one of the pioneers in the design and production of digital signal microprocessors. The TMS320 family includes an MOS microprocessor capable of executing five million instructions per second. This high throughput is the result of the comprehensive, efficient, and easily programmed instruction set and of the highly pipelined architecture. Special instructions, such as multiply/accumulate with fast data move, have been incorporated in the TMS320 family to speed execution of digital signal processing algorithms. A comprehensive general-purpose instruction set also is included. For example, the branch instructions encompass all of the various conditions of the accumulator. Three different addressing modes are provided – direct, indirect, and immediate. A full set of Boolean instructions exists for testing bits. Bit extractions and interrupt capabilities also are features of the TMS320 processor.

The TMS320 family displays a modified Harvard architecture. In a pure Harvard architecture, separate program and data memories are used. In the TMS320 family, the architecture allows transfer between program and data spaces, thereby increasing the flexibility of these devices. This architectural modification eliminates the need for a separate coefficient ROM and also maximizes power by maintaining two separate bus structures – i.e., program and data, for full-speed execution.

The TMS320 family of digital signal processors is listed in Fig. 7–1. A brief description of these processors follows.

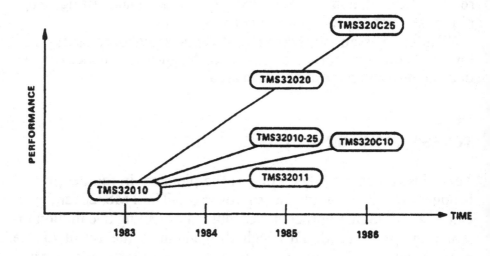

Fig. 7-1. TMS320 family of digital signal processors

Texas Instruments also provides for this family of digital signal processors a number of software development tools, such as a macro assembler/linker and digital filter design software.

TMS32010 and TMS320C10 Digital Signal Processors

The TMS32010 digital signal processor is a first-generation device, which implements in hardware many functions that other processors typically perform in software.

The architecture of the TMS32010 is shown in Fig. 7–2. The device contains a hardware multiplier that performs a 16 x 16-bit multiplication, providing a 32-bit product in a single 200-nanosecond cycle. A hardware barrel shifter is used to shift data on its way into the arithmetic-logic unit. Extra hardware has been included to allow auxiliary registers to be configured in an auto-increment/decrement mode for single-cycle manipulation of data tables. These auxiliary registers provide indirect data RAM addresses.

The TMS32010 is equipped with 1536-word mask-programmed ROM. The device also can execute at full speed from an additional 2560 words of off-chip program memory. This memory expansion capability is particularly useful for applications that share subroutines. In these cases, common subroutines can be stored on-chip while the application-specific code is stored off-chip.

The TMS320C10 is a CMOS replica of the TMS32010. Both devices display essentially the same characteristic — that is, an instruction cycle time of 200 nanoseconds at 20 Mhz. However, because of low power consumption (100 milliwatts), the CMOS version is particularly suitable for power-sensitive applications, such as digital telephony and portable consumer products.

TMS32011 Digital Signal Processor

The TMS32011 digital signal processor is a slightly modified version of the TMS32010. The '011 is equipped with a 1.5-Kword, on-chip ROM and has no external memory expansion capability — i.e., it lacks an external address bus. The '011 includes two on-chip, serial ports. In addition, pulse code modulation (PCM) companding functions and a timer have been implemented in hardware to reduce the program memory size and to increase the CPU utilization for applica-

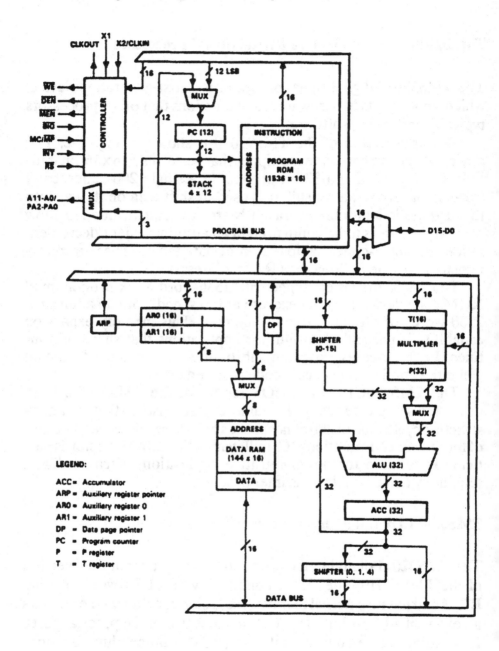

Fig. 7-2. Architecture of the TMS32010

tions using codecs.

TMS32010–25 Digital Signal Processor

The TMS32010–25 is a faster version (160-ns cycle time) of the TMS32010. This version is intended for higher performance applications using off-chip memory. These types of applications require a processor throughput of 6.25 million instructions per second, which is 25% more than the generic TMS32010 can provide.

TMS32020 and TMS320C25 Digital Signal Processors

The TMS32020 is a second-generation device. It significantly enhances the memory spaces of the processor, providing 544 words of on-chip data and program memories. Increased throughput is accomplished by means of single-cycle multiply/accumulate instructions with a data move option, five auxiliary registers with a dedicated arithmetic unit, and faster input-output, necessary for data-intensive operations. The processor has 109 instructions, including special repeat instructions for streamlining program space and execution time.

Fig. 7–3 shows the architecture of the TMS32020. Some of the key features of this device are:

1. 544 words of on-chip data RAM;
2. 128 Kwords of memory space, divided into equal-sized program and data memories;
3. single-cycle multiply/accumulate instructions;
4. repeat instructions;
5. 200-ns instruction cycle;
6. a serial port for multiprocessing or codec interface;
7. 16 input and 16 output channels;
8. a 16-bit parallel interface;
9. a directly accessible external data memory space;

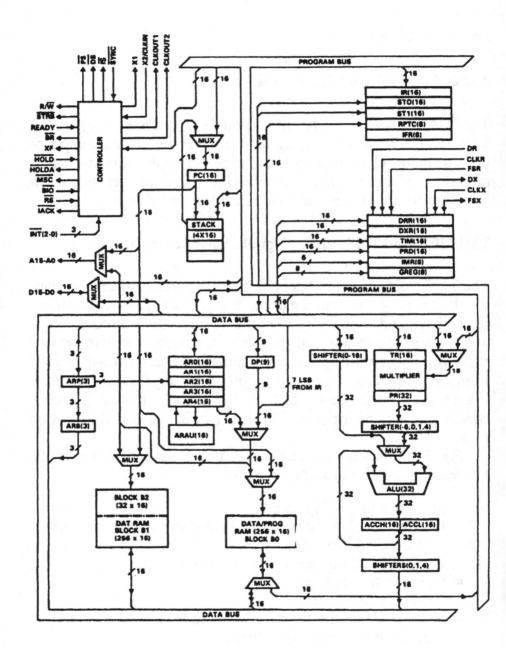

Fig. 7-3. Architecture of the TMS32020

10. global data memory interface;
11. block moves for data/program memories;
12. instruction set support for floating-point operations; and
13. upward software compatibility with the generic processor.

The TMS320C25 digital signal processor is a pin-compatible CMOS version of the TMS32020. However, the '025 has additional hardware characteristics that enhance processor speed, system integration, and ease of application development. The instruction cycle time of the '025 is 100 ns. More instructions have been added. Additional on-chip hardware, such as an eight-deep hardware stack and eight auxiliary registers, results in two to three times the throughput of the generic device. The presence of a large on-chip masked ROM (4 Kwords) makes the '025 ideal for single-chip applications, thus reducing power, cost, and board space.

The architecture of the TMS320C25 is shown in Fig. 7–4.

WE DSP32 (AT&T) DIGITAL SIGNAL PROCESSOR

The WE DSP32 is a 32-bit, high-speed, mask-programmable, digital signal processor with uses in speech recognition, high-speed modems, very-low-bit-rate speech codecs, and multichannel signaling systems.

The architecture of the WE DSP32 is shown in Fig. 7–5. The device consists of: a data arithmetic unit (DAU); a control arithmetic unit (CAU); parallel and serial input-output; and on-chip ROM and RAM.

Data Arithmetic Unit

The data arithmetic unit is the main computing element of the DSP32. The unit contains a 32-bit floating-point multiplier, a 40-bit floating-point adder, a data arithmetic unit control register, and four

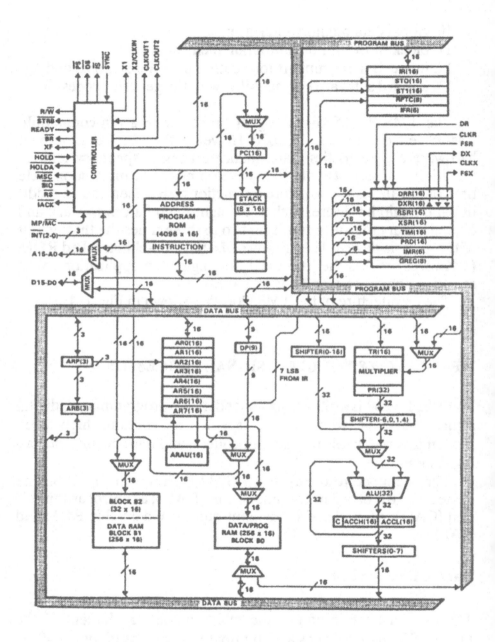

Fig. 7-4. Architecture of the TMS320C25

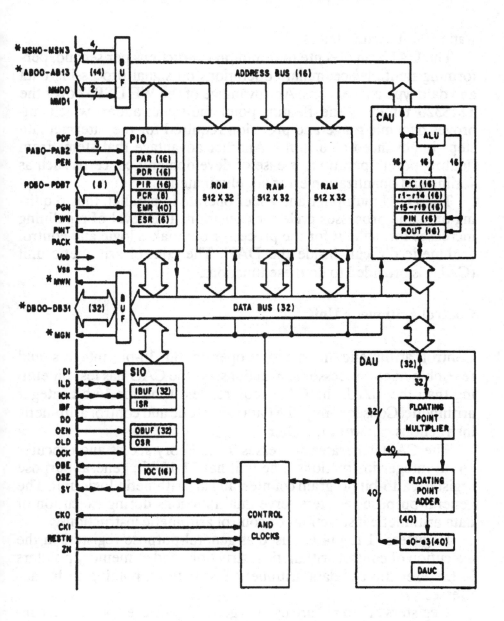

Fig. 7-5. Architecture of the WE DSP32
digital signal processor

static 40-bit accumulators.

The DAU can execute four million instructions per second, performing multiply/accumulate operations on signal processing data and data type conversions. An advantage of the WE DSP32 over the TMS320 family is the floating-point multiplier/adder, which improves dynamic range and precision required for the intermediate steps in advanced algorithms. Another advantage that stems from floating-point operations is ease of development; concerns such as scaling and quantization error are eliminated.

The DAU multiplier and adder operate in parallel, thus requiring only one processor cycle for execution. This level of pipelining increases throughput for the processor but makes logic and control arithmetic difficult inside the DAU. The control arithmetic unit (CAU) is provided to do these functions.

Control Arithmetic Unit

Control arithmetic instructions operate on 16-bit integers and resemble microprocessor instructions. As the CAU has less pipelining than the DAU, the CAU requires less time for 16-bit integer arithmetic. Consequently, the data arithmetic and control arithmetic instructions can work together.

The CAU generates addresses for memory access and executes 16-bit integer instructions. The unit has 21 16-bit, general-purpose registers, a 16-bit program counter, and an arithmetic-logic unit. The general-purpose registers serve dual functions during execution of data arithmetic instructions or control arithmetic instructions.

Registers r1 to r14 are used as general-purpose registers in the execution of control arithmetic instructions and as memory pointers in the execution of data arithmetic instructions, holding 16-bit addresses.

Registers r15 to r19 are used as general-purpose registers in control arithmetic instructions and as increment registers in data arithmetic instructions, holding values that postmodify addresses that the memory pointers hold.

Register r20, called *Pointer-In* (PIN), is used as the serial input-output direct-memory access input pointer. Register r21, called *Pointer-Out* (POUT), is used as the serial input-output direct-memory access output pointer.

Memory

The DSP32 is equipped with 2 Kbytes and 4 Kbytes of on-chip ROM and RAM, respectively. Typically, instructions and fixed operands are stored in ROM, and variable operands are stored in RAM.

Memory can be expanded off-chip, up to 56 Kbytes.

Serial and Parallel Input-Output

Serial communication between the DSP32 and external devices is accomplished via the SIO and a double-buffering configuration. Double buffering facilitates back-to-back transfers. That is, a serial transmission can begin before a previous transmission has been completed. Data widths of 8, 16, and 32 bits can be selected.

The parallel input-output consists of three 16-bit registers — PAR, PDR, and PIR, a 10-bit register — EMR, an 8-bit register — PCR, and a 6-bit register — ESR. Bidirectional data transfers between the 8-bit parallel i/o data bus and the DSP32 proceed through the parallel data register (PDR).

INMOS A100 DIGITAL SIGNAL PROCESSOR

INMOS, the manufacturer of the Transputer, also is in the digital signal processing business. These devices, however, are configurable rather than programmable. For example, although a complete system could be built using only the A100 device (one-dimensional filtering) or A110 devices (image processing), the design of these devices is such that multiple devices can be used in conjunction with a controlling microprocessor. This arrangement of controlling microprocessor and arrayable function/algorithm-specific device maintains the flexibility of a programmable system, but allows very high performance in a small number of devices.

IMS A100 Cascadable Signal Processor

This device is essentially a 32-stage, cascadable, digital transversal filter. The general canonical transversal filter is shown in Fig. 7–6a, and an alternative, and functionally equivalent, filter is shown in Fig. 7–6b. This alternative is the building block for the IMS A100, to which the input signal is supplied in parallel to all 32 multipliers, and the delay and summation operations are performed in a distributed manner.

(a)

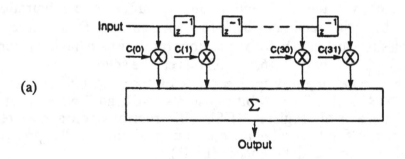

(b)

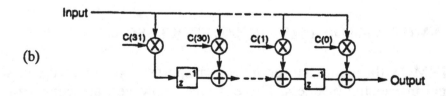

Fig. 7-6. (a) Canonical transversal filter architecture;
(b) modified transversal filter architecture

The internal architecture of the IMS A100 is depicted in Fig. 7–7. The device has four interfaces through which data can be transferred. The memory interface port allows access to the coefficient registers, the configuration and status registers, and the data input and output registers for the multiplier accumulator array. Three dedicated ports also are provided, allowing high-speed data input and output to the IMS and the cascading of several devices.

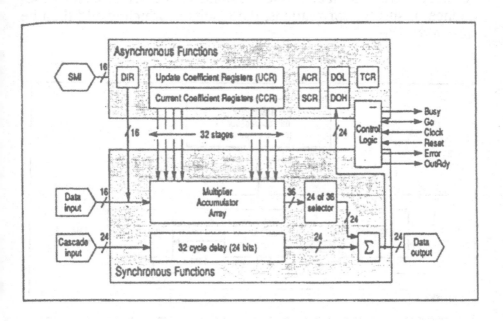

Fig. 7-7. Internal architecture of the IMS A100

A microprocessor can be connected to the IMS A100 via the memory interface (SMI), and, in a simple system, data input and output can be performed through the data-input register (DIR) and data-output register (DOL, DOH). In a high-performance configuration, a microprocessor can be connected to the IMS A100 via the dedicated input and output ports.

A typical simple system appears in Fig. 7–8. A price-performance tradeoff must be paid for the advantage of cascading. For example, a correlation application could achieve high performance by using a cascade of IMS A100s sufficiently long to hold one of the waveforms being correlated in its coefficient registers and sending the other waveform involved in the correlation along the cascade of IMS A100s. A cheaper but slower solution would be to use a smaller number of A100s and to decompose the single long correlation into a sequence of shorter correlations, the results of which would then be summed.

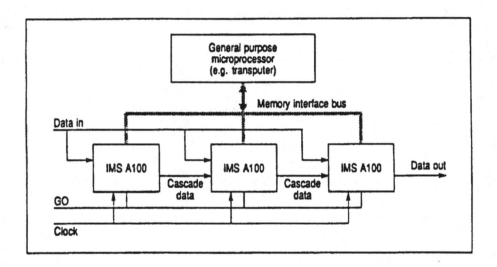

Fig. 7-8. A simple IMS A100-based system

IMS A110 Image and Signal Processing Subsystem

The A110 consists of a configurable array of multiply accumulators, three programmable-length 1120 stage shift registers, a versatile postprocessing unit, and a microprocessor interface for configuration and control purposes. The comprehensive on-chip facilities make a single device capable of dealing with many image processing operations. Figure 7–9 depicts the architecture of the A110.

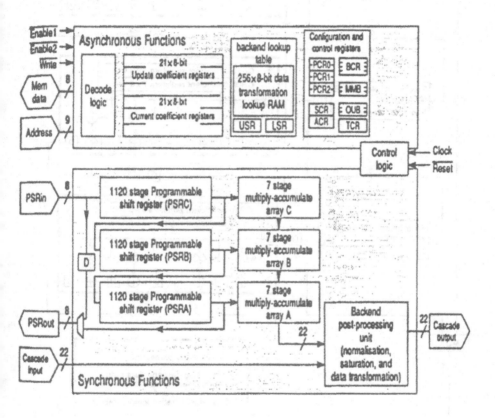

Fig. 7-9. Architecture of the A110 signal processor

As shown in Fig. 7–10, the processing core of the device comprises a configurable array of multiple accumulators (mac). The mac array has three seven-stage, transversal filters that can be configured either

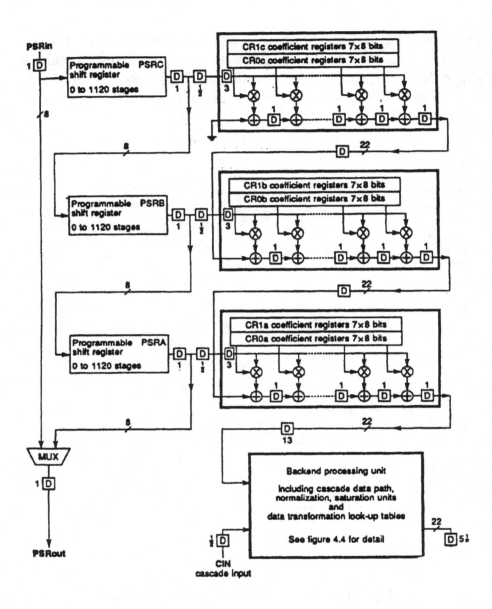

Fig. 7-10. Synchronous functions of the A110

as a 21-stage linear pipeline or as a 3 x 7 two-dimensional window. The input data are 8 bits wide and are fed to the mac array via three programmable shift registers.

The output of each shift register is supplied as input to one of the three seven-stage transversal filters. The data associated with each filter are fed simultaneously to all seven mac stages. At each stage, the input sample is multiplied by a coefficient stored in memory and added to the output of the previous stage delayed by one clock cycle. The output of each seven-stage mac is fed, via a delay stage, to the first stage in the next transver sal filter.

A typical A110-based system is set forth in Fig. 7–11.

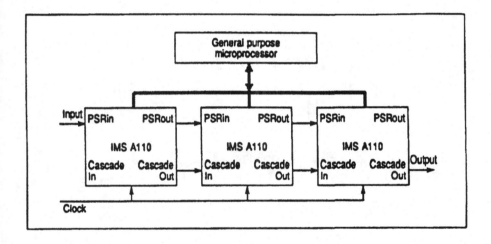

Fig. 7-11. Typical A110 system

TEXAS INSTRUMENTS' TMS34010 GRAPHICS PROCESSOR

The TMS34010 is an advanced 32-bit microprocessor, optimized for graphics systems. The device is the building block for numerous applications, such as terminals, laser printers, and engineering workstations.

Figure 7–12 illustrates the architecture of the TMS34010 and its interface to external devices. Special processing hardware includes:

1. hardware for detecting whether a pixel lies within a specific window;
2. hardware for detecting the leftmost one in a 32-bit register; and
3. hardware for expanding a black-and-white pattern to a variable pixel-depth pattern.

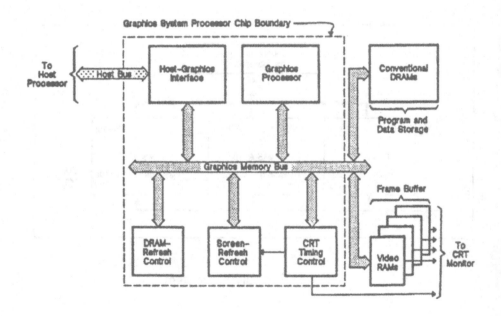

Fig. 7-12. Architecture of the TMS34010

The instruction set provides several fundamental graphics operations. Two-dimensional pixel arrays can be manipulated. A pixel can be drawn and its address can be incremented by a specific value; thus, circles, ellipses, arcs, and other curves can be drawn easily. A pixel-transfer instruction tranfers individual pixels from one location to another.

SUMMARY

This chapter describes various classes of signal and image processors. These devices are particularly useful in speech and handwriting recognition and graphics. Most of the devices have sophisticated features that cannot be described fully in this book because of its size limitations. The brief descriptions of the devices, however, afford a fair idea of their qualities.

Chapter 8
Microprocessors and Multiprocessing

GENERAL

Multiprocessing, previously a rather expensive task, now can be performed cheaply and efficiently by microprocessors. But what is multiprocessing? Intepretation of this term is frequently confusing. In a general sense, multiprocessing is the use of a number of processors to carry out a single task, partitioned into subtasks and usually executed at the same time. Assume, for example, that an application requires a throughput equivalent to a microprocessor operating at a clock rate of 60 MHz. Such a device would be hard to find and quite costly to construct. If, however, the application is divided into, say, 10 subtasks, each of which is executed concurrently by 10 different microprocessors, an effectively high throughput results. This, of course, is only a rough definition of multiprocessing.

Many problems need to be solved before a multiprocessing system can function successfully. One problem is "deadlock," in which, for example, a microprocessor refuses to give up an i/o port that it has been using. There is also "starvation," in which unequal distribution of data among microprocessors results in one microprocessor getting all data and another getting no data at all—i.e., starving. Yet another problem is the interconnection, or topology, of microprocessors; not all topologies are suitable for the solution of all problems. Another problem is the management of memory resources.

Notwithstanding the problems, advantages do accrue from multimicroprocessing in terms of economy, reliability, fault tolerance, and flexibility.

Consider economy. The cost of computer hardware lies almost

221

entirely in its memory and peripherals. Often the microprocessor itself represents no more than 0.01% to 1% of the retail price of a system. Therefore, addition of more microprocessors has little effect on the overall cost of a system, provided, naturally, that they share the same resources. Even with the addition of extra resources, however, a multimicroprocessing system now costs far less that multiprocessors of previous generations.

Reliability may be computed with a simple equation. If the probability of failure of a processor over a given time is p, then the probability of simultaneous failure of two processors is p^2. Thus, if p is 1% per 10^4 hours for a given microprocessor, reliability of a two-processor system is 0.01% per 10^4 hours, and reliability of a three-processor system is 0.0001% per 10^4. One, of course, must consider also the reliability of the other components in a system.

A so-called fault-tolerant system, in which one or two subsystems may fail but the overall performance of the total system will not suffer appreciably, is feasible. To accomplish a low mean-time-between-failures, however, such a system may employ either massive or selective redundancy.

"Reconfigurable" multiprocessors may be classified under the advantage of flexibility. If one processor subsystem fails, the total system may be refigured to remove the failed processor from the chain.

Reconfigurable multiprocessors are also suitable for some applications in which a specific topology is of importance, although for other applications such multiprocessors are not.

Topologies of multimicroprocessors have been cited previously as a problem. Examine some of the typical topologies.

TOPOLOGIES

Topology, or interconnection, has several important parameters — average distance, communication links, routing algorithm, fault-tolerance, and expansion.

Average distance is the distance that messages must travel, on the average, in a given topology. Average distance is given by:

$$AvgDist = \frac{\displaystyle\sum_{d=1}^{r} dN_d}{N-1}$$

where N_d is the number of processors at a distance d links away, r is the diameter (maximum of the minimum distance between any two pairs of nodes), and N is the total number of processors.

Normalized average distance is a related term used for a network that has a low average distance and may require an unreasonable number of communication links for each processor. This term is given by:

Norm Avg Dist (link) = Avg Dist x Ports/Processor

where Ports/processor is the number of communication ports required of each processor. The term on the right-hand side of the equation can be modified slightly for use with bus structures. Thus,

Norm Avg Dist (bus) = Avg Dist x Ports/bus.

Communication links are another useful measure of the performance of a topology. The fewer connecting links, the better.

A routing algorithm prescribes the route that a message must take on its way from one processor to another. It is desirable for the algorithm to be simple and not to require complete knowledge of the entire topology. It is particularly convenient if, by merely having the destination address, it is possible to obtain the exact — and preferably the shortest — sequence of processors through which a message must travel.

Fault tolerance has been discussed previously, and its advantages are evident.

A well-designed large system must be capable of expansion. This expansion, however, must be accomplished in a manner that creates a minimum of disruption of the overall system.

Topologies are classified into two categories — i.e., link-oriented networks and bus-oriented networks.

Link-Oriented Networks

Ring Topology. In a ring topology, as shown in Fig. 8–1a, a processor is connected only to its nearest neighbor. This simple topology has simple routing and is very popular in local-area networks. The average distance is $(N+1)/4$, where N is odd. The normalized average distance is $(N+1)/2$, as each processor provides two ports.

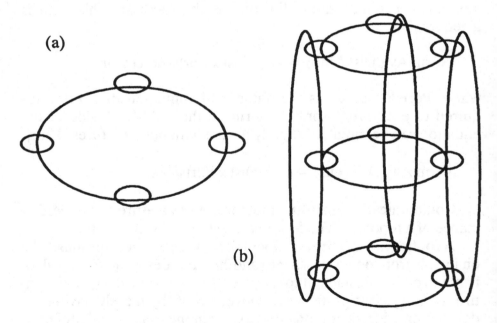

(a)

(b)

Fig. 8-1. (a) The ring topology; (b) two-dimensional
ring topology with nine processors

The total number of communication links in the ring topology is N. The routing algorithm is fairly straightforward, simplest for uni-directional rings and slightly more complex for bidirectional rings.

Due to the simplicity of a ring, its fault-tolerant features are questionable. If a ring becomes large in terms of processors, then the normalized average distance becomes unacceptably large. In unidirectional rings, failure of just one processor may render the entire ring inoperative. In bidirectional rings, failure of two nodes will cause a malfunction. At the same time, this simplicity enables a ring topology to expand very easily.

Cube-Connected Cycles. This type of network connects 2^k computers (k is an integer) in such a way that groups of 2^r (r is the smallest integer such that $r + 2 = >k$) are interconnected so as to form a ($k - r$)-dimension cube. Each component has a k-bit address that is expressed as a pair of integers (l, p), l having ($k - r$) bits, and p having r bits.

There are three ports, called F, B, and L (for forward, backward, and lateral), on each computer, and the interconnection rules are:

$F(l, p)$ connected to $B(l, (p + 1) \bmod 2^r)$;
$B(l, p)$ connected to $F(l, (p-1) \bmod 2^r)$; and
$L(l, p)$ connected to $L(l + e^p)$;

where $e = 1 - 2 \times (p^{th}$ bit of l).

Figure 8–2 depicts a cube-connected cycles topology (CCC).

The average distance of the CCC is the product of the average distance of the subgroup of 2^r processors, which form a ring, and the main ($k - r$)-cube network. The number of ports in each computer is 3, so the normalized distance is simply the average distance times 3.

The total number of communication links is at most $(3/2)N$, where N is the total number of nodes in the network.

There are simple routing algorithms available for this topology. Even when a node is faulty, an alternative path may be found easily.

Due to its cube structure, the CCC cannot be expanded easily. Not only must the expansion be in powers of 2, but the system must be completely restructured.

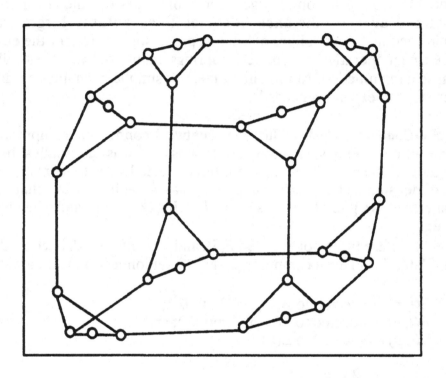

Fig. 8-2. Cube-connected cycles typology

Alpha Network. An alpha network topology is a generalized hypercube structure. Unlike the hypercube, which needs the number of nodes to be of the form $N = W^W$, the alpha network is valid for all nonprime values of N.

The alpha network is constructed in the following manner:

Let $m_1, m_2, ..., m_d$ be chosen such that m_i is integer and

$$\prod_{i=1}^{d} m_i = N$$

Each node then can be expressed in a mixed radix form as a d-tuple $(x_d, x_{d-1}, ..., x_1)$ that forms the address of a node. Connections are made from each node to every node whose address differs by 1 in any one coordinate. Such a topology is illustrated in Fig. 8–3.

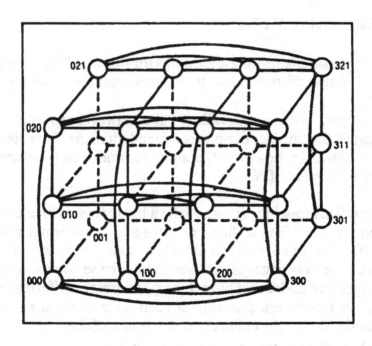

Fig. 8-3. A 4 x 4 x 3 alpha network

The average distance of the alpha network is given by:

$$\text{Avg Dist (alpha)} = \frac{D\,(W-1)\,W^{N-1}}{N-1}$$

The number of ports provided by each processor is given by:

Ports(alpha) = $D(W-1)$.

The total number of communication links is:

Links(alpha) = N x Ports/2.

There are simple routing algorithms for this topology. Due to the presence of several redundant paths, this topology is highly fault-tolerant.

As this network is a generalized cube network, expansion is not easy because the number of ports is dependent on network size. Unlike cube networks, however, the alpha network can accommodate any nonprime value of N.

Hypertree. This topology is essentially a binary tree with a carefully designed topology. The addition of extra edges that connect sibling nodes offers a small average distance and a measure of fault-tolerance. The new edges are chosen to be n-cube connections; that is, the edges link nodes that have (binary) addresses differing by only one bit. Four ports are available at each node—i.e., one from the parent node, two to the children, and one to a sibling.

The hypertree topology is shown in Fig. 8–4.

The objective of this topology is to decrease the distance between nodes. For example, the distance between nodes 9 and 14 is 4. Therefore, the siblings are chosen to reduce this distance. Table 8–1 shows the distances in Fig. 8–4. An entry in the ith row and j^{th} column of the table provides the distance between those siblings in the $(i + 1)^{th}$ row whose addresses differ in the jth bit position. A circled entry represents the maximum for that row. Entries just below a circled entry are not considered, because, in effect, they are reduced to three by the sibling links in the previous level. Entries two rows below the circled entry are reduced to five, and so on. The table assists in the selection of sibling links since, for every level i, links are given by the value of the circled entry in the table.

The total number of communication links is given by $N + 2(2^{\lceil \log_2 N \rceil - 1} - 1)$.

This topology is easily expandable with minimal disruption to the remaining system.

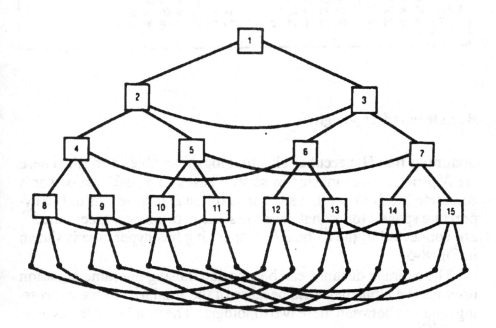

Fig. 8-4. A hypertree topology

Table 8-1.

MSB	Nonequivalent node address bit →																			LSB
00001	02																			
00010	04	02																		
00011	06	04	02																	
00100	08	06	04	02																
00101	10	08	06	04	02															
00110	12	10	08	06	04	02														
00111	14	12	10	08	06	04	02													
01000	16	14	12	10	08	06	04	02												
01001	18	16	14	12	10	08	06	04	02											
01010	20	18	16	14	12	10	08	06	04	02										
01011	22	20	18	16	14	12	10	08	06	04	02									
01100	24	22	20	18	16	14	12	10	08	06	04	02								
01101	26	24	22	20	18	16	14	12	10	08	06	04	02							
01110	28	26	24	22	20	18	16	14	12	10	08	06	04	02						
01111	30	28	26	24	22	20	18	16	14	12	10	08	06	04	02					
10000	32	30	28	26	24	22	20	18	16	14	12	10	08	06	04	02				
10001	34	32	30	28	26	24	22	20	18	16	14	12	10	08	06	04	02			
10010	36	34	32	30	28	26	24	22	20	18	16	14	12	10	08	06	04	02		
10011	38	36	34	32	30	28	26	24	22	20	18	16	14	12	10	08	06	04	02	
10100	40	38	36	34	32	30	28	26	24	22	20	18	16	14	12	10	08	06	04	02

Bus-Oriented Topologies

Spanning Bus Hypercube. This topology resembles a mesh. There are N processors connected by several buses – i.e., each processor is connected to D buses that span each of the D dimensions of the hypercube space. Nodes that have the same coordinates, except the ith, are connected to the ith bus. A 3^3 spanning bus hypercube is shown in Fig. 8–5.

The average distance can be calculated using the same equation used for the alpha network, because of the similarity in the addressing schemes between these two topologies. The number of buses used is DW^{D-1}

The network can be expanded by increasing D or W.

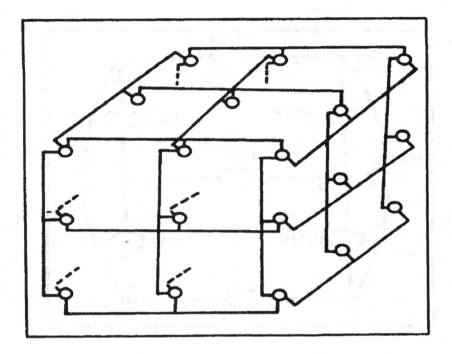

Fig. 8-5. A 3^3 spanning hypercube network

Beta Topology. This network also is similar to the alpha network, except that, in the latter, a link is substituted for a node (processor) in the beta topology. The node of the alpha network is a bus in the beta network. Figure 8–6 shows a 2 x 3 beta network.

The number of buses is given as W^D. The number of nodes is given by:

$$N = \frac{W^D(W-1)}{2}$$

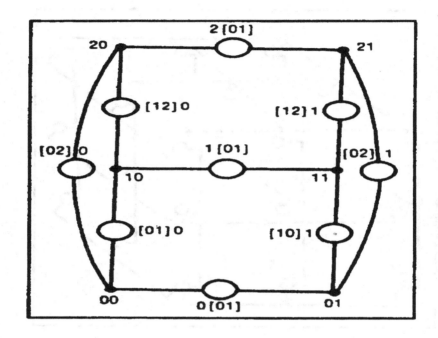

Fig. 8-6. A 2 x 3 beta network

There are several other topologies, and some are given as examples in the following case study. These topologies include the mesh and butterfly networks.

CASE STUDY OF MULTIPROCESSING WITH THE TRANSPUTER

INMOS produces a four-transputer board, called the B003, that can be used to create multiprocessor systems. Figure 8–7 shows that the internal configuration of the B003 is a ring topology. Nonetheless, with the B003, a wide variety of topologies is possible.

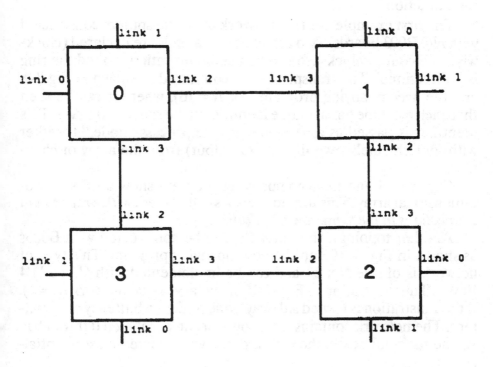

Fig. 8-7. Ring configuration of the B003 transputer board

In general, in each configuration, arrays of channels are declared, and each channel within these arrays is placed at two link addresses (one input and one output) of two different transputers that are connected to each other.

The appropriate index for the array, like a mapping index, is a function of the machine identifier. A mapping array that contains a list of link addresses also is declared for input and output channels. The mapping index is used to reference these arrays so that a channel can be placed at the correct link address. Placed in this way, channels then can be passed as parameters to the system call procedure for extraction.

The first example is a ring network of N transputers constructed with $N/4$ B003 boards. Two arrays of N channels are declared (clockwise and counterclockwise), so that communication around the ring is bidirectional. The transputers are connected as shown in Fig 8–8 and the accompanying program (for $N = 16$), where it can be seen that each machine has a unique identifier in the range of $0...N\text{-}1$. This identifier is passed as a parameter to the process "node," together with four channels (two input, two output) from the array of channels.

Figure 8–9 and its accompanying program show an 8 x 8 two-dimensional array. This topology also is called *mesh with wraparound connections in the same row or column.*

Another topology, the butterfly, can be constructed with B003s as shown in Fig. 8–10 and the accompanying program. This type of network is of size $N \times 2^N$ and can be implemented with $(N \times 2^N)/4$ B003s. The illustration in Fig. 8–10 shows a 64-node network ($n = 4$). If the illustration is turned sideways, one notices a butterfly wing pattern. The network contains $k + 1$ rows, or ranks, labeled 0 through k. As the ranks decrease, the widths of the wings increase exponentially.

In the diagram in Fig. 8–10, four arrays of channels of dimension "nodes" (number of transputers in the network) are declared: adj.left, adj.right, diag.left, and diag.right, where "adj" is a mnemonic for adjacent connection and "diag" is a mnemonic for diagonal connection. This configuration enables the transputer to send or receive data to or from any of its four neighbors. Eight placed channels (four input, four output) are passed to the system call procedure "node."

The final network in this case study is an $N \times 2^N$ cube-connected cycle constructed with $N \times 2^N/4$ B003s, where again $N = 4$. Three arrays of channels are declared of dimension "nodes" (number of transputers in the network): clockwise.route, counterclockwise.route, and cross.route, where "clockwise" and "counterclockwise" represent channels connected to nodes in the same row, and "cross" represents a channel connected to a different row. See Fig. 8–11 and the accompanying program.

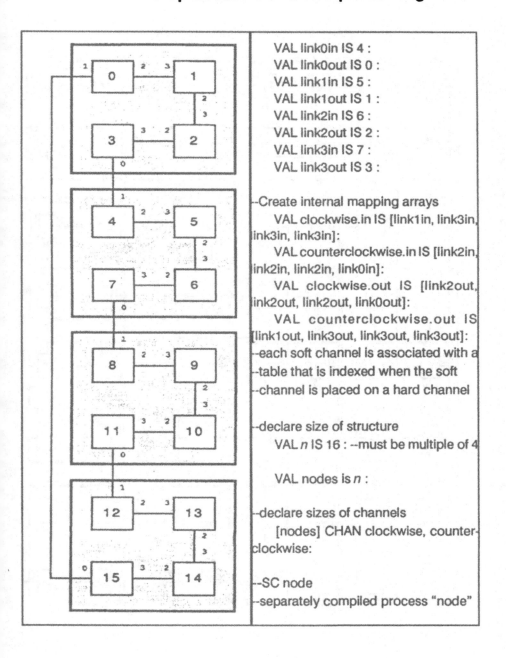

VAL link0in IS 4 :
VAL link0out IS 0 :
VAL link1in IS 5 :
VAL link1out IS 1 :
VAL link2in IS 6 :
VAL link2out IS 2 :
VAL link3in IS 7 :
VAL link3out IS 3 :

--Create internal mapping arrays
    VAL clockwise.in IS [link1in, link3in, link3in, link3in]:
    VAL counterclockwise.in IS [link2in, link2in, link2in, link0in]:
    VAL clockwise.out IS [link2out, link2out, link2out, link0out]:
    VAL counterclockwise.out IS [link1out, link3out, link3out, link3out]:
--each soft channel is associated with a
--table that is indexed when the soft
--channel is placed on a hard channel

--declare size of structure
    VAL n IS 16 : --must be multiple of 4

    VAL nodes is n :

--declare sizes of channels
    [nodes] CHAN clockwise, counter-clockwise:

--SC node
--separately compiled process "node"

Fig. 8-8. 16-node ring   Program for Fig. 8–8

Fig. 8-9. 8 x 8 wraparound mesh topology

```
    VAL link0in IS 4:
    VAL link0out IS 0:
    VAL link1in IS 5:
    VAL link1out IS 1:
    VAL link2in IS 6:
    VAL link2out IS 2:
    VAL link3in IS 7:
    VAL link3out IS 3:

--create internal mapping arrays
    VAL left.to.right.in IS [link0in, link3in, link1in, link2in]:
    VAL right.to.left.in IS [link2in, link1in, link3in, link0in]:
    VAL top.to.bottom.in IS [link1in, link0in, link2in, link3in]:
    VAL bottom.to.top.in IS [link3in, link2in, link0in, link1in]:
    VAL left.to.right.out IS [link2out, link1out, link3out, link0out]:
    VAL right.to.left.out IS [link0out, link3out, link1out, link2out]:
    VAL top.to.bottom.out IS [link3out, link2out, link0out, link1out]:
    VAL bottom.to.top.out IS [link1out, link0out, link2out, link3out]:
--each soft channel is associated with a table that is indexed when the soft
--channel is placed on a hard channel

--declare size of structure
    VAL n IS 8:
    VAL p IS n:  --x dimension of array
    VAL q IS n:  -- y dimension of array
    VAL nodes IS p * q:

--declare sizes of channels
    [nodes]CHAN left.to.right,
    right.to.left,
    top.to.bottom,
    bottom.to.top:

--SC node
--separately compiled process "node" to be extracted to all nodes
```

Program for Fig. 8-9

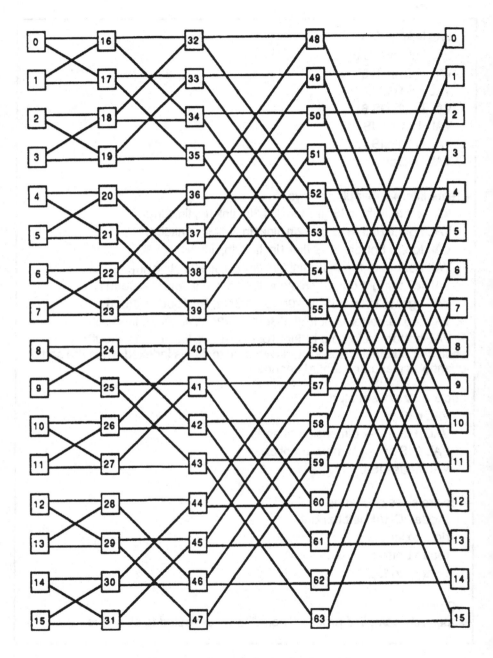

Fig. 8-10. 64-node butterfly network

```
    VAL link0in IS 4:
    VAL link0out IS 0:
    VAL link1in IS 5:
    VAL link1out IS 1:
    VAL link2in IS 6:
    VAL link2out IS 2:
    VAL link3in IS 7:
    VAL link3out IS 3:

--create internal mapping arrays
    VAL adj.left.in IS [link2in, link0in, link2in, link0in]:
    VAL adj.right.in IS [link1in, link3in, link1in, link3in]:
    VAL diag.left.in IS [link3in, link1in, link3in, link1in]:
    VAL diag.right.in IS [link0in, link2in, link0in, link2in]:
    VAL adj.left.out IS [link1out, link3out, link1out, link3out]:
    VAL adj.right.out IS [link2out, link0out, link2out, link0out]:
    VAL diag.left.out IS [link0out, link2out, link0out, link2out]:
    VAL diag.right.out IS [link3out, link1out, link3out, link1out]:
--each soft channel is associated with a table that is indexed when the soft
-- channel is placed on a hard channel

--declare size of structure
    VAL n IS 4:
    VAL p IS n,   --width of FBS (minimum of 2)
        q IS (1 < <n): --height of FBS
    VAL nodes IS p * q

--declare sizes of channels
[nodes] CHAN adj.left,   --adj = adjacent connection
               adj.right,  --diag = diagonal connection
               diag.left,   --left = right to left direction
               diag.right:  -- right = left to right direction

SC node
--separately compiled process "node" to be extracted to all nodes
```

Program for Fig. 8-10

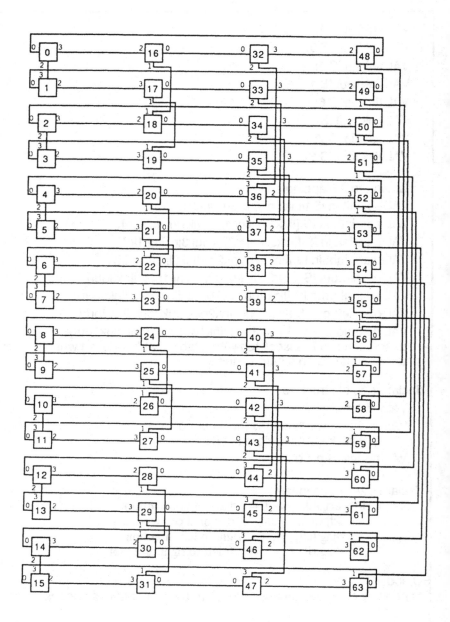

Fig. 8-11. 64-node cube-connected cycle

```
      VAL link0in IS 4:
      VAL link0out IS 0:
      VAL link1in IS 5:
      VAL link1out IS 1:
      VAL link2in IS 6:
      VAL link2out IS 2:
      VAL link3in IS 7:
      VAL link3out IS 3:

--declare size of structure

      VAL p IS 6,  --width of CCC (minimum is 2)
          q IS (1 < <p):  --height of CCC
      VAL nodes IS p * q:

--declare sizes of channels

[nodes] CHAN clockwise.route, --clockwise cycle links
      counterclockwise.route, --counterclockwise cycle links
      cross.route :  --cross links to other dimensions

--create internal mappings

      VAL clockwise.in.map IS [link0in, link0in, link2in, link3in]:
      VAL counterclockwise.in.map IS [link3in, link2in, link0in, link0in]:
      VAL cross.in.map IS [link2in, link3in, link1in, link1in]:
      VAL clockwise.out.map IS [link3out, link2out, link0out, link0out]:
      VAL counterclockwise.out.map IS [link0out, link0out, link2out, link3out]:
      VAL cross.out.map IS [link2out, link3out, link1out, link1out]:

--each soft channel has a table that is indexed when the soft channel is placed
--on a hard channel


--SC node

--separately compiled process to be extraced to all nodes
```

Program for Fig. 8-11

This case certainly verifies the versatility of the Transputer.

SUMMARY

Various topologies for multimicroprocessor systems are described in this chapter. There are many areas of commerce, industry, and science where high performance is always required and multiprocessing, accomplished in an efficient and cost-effective manner, is certainly in demand. One of the microprocessors suitable for multiprocessing, as the case study has shown, is the Transputer.

INDEX

Index